ARROYO CENTER

The U.S. Department of Defense's Planning Process

Components and Challenges

Michael J. Mazarr, Katharina Ley Best, Burgess Laird, Eric V. Larson, Michael E. Linick, Dan Madden

Prepared for the United States Army

Approved for public release; distribution unlimited

For more information on this publication, visit www.rand.org/t/RR2173z2

Library of Congress Cataloging-in-Publication Data is available for this publication.
ISBN: 978-0-8330-9990-7

Published by the RAND Corporation, Santa Monica, Calif.
© Copyright 2019 RAND Corporation
RAND® is a registered trademark.

Cover: Photo by Angel_a/Getty Images

Support RAND
Make a tax-deductible charitable contribution at
www.rand.org/giving/contribute

www.rand.org

Preface

This report documents research and analysis conducted as part of Phase Two of a project titled *Defense Planning for a New Era*, sponsored by Headquarters, Department of the Army, G-8, Army Quadrennial Defense Review Office. Phase Two of this project is focused on outlining a framework for defense planning and force-sizing for the 2018 Defense Strategy Review, including planning scenarios that represent the full range of likely and potential operational demands for U.S. Army forces, both domestically and overseas. Phase Two also describes the current defense planning process used by the U.S. Department of Defense (DoD), with a focus on how scenarios are developed and employed to support defense planning. It examines and critiques the way scenarios are used in current planning processes, based on an assessment of unclassified documents and dialogues with current and former participants in the process.

This document was preceded by a report that covered Phase One of the project and described the forces that shaped conventional ground force planning during the 1945–2015 period, with a focus on the strategic concepts and contingency scenarios used, and also identified broader lessons of likely interest to contemporary force planners.[1]

The third phase of the project will turn to a substantive analysis of the Army that the nation needs, offering a framework for evaluating the current scenario set in ways that provide insight on current Army choices and trade-offs.

This research should be of interest to those directly involved in the Army and the wider DoD defense planning process, including senior Army leaders concerned with the broadest questions of Army roles and missions.

The Project Unique Identification Code (PUIC) for the project that produced this document is HQD157136.

This research was conducted within RAND Arroyo Center's Strategy, Doctrine, and Resources Program. RAND Arroyo Center, part of the RAND Corporation, is a federally funded research and development center (FFRDC) sponsored by the United States Army.

---

[1] Eric V. Larson, *Force Planning Scenarios, 1945–2016: Their Origins and Use in Defense Strategic Planning,* Santa Monica, Calif.: RAND Corporation, RR-2173-A, forthcoming.

Contents

Figures and Table

Figures

Table

Summary

The U.S. Department of Defense (DoD) relies on planning processes to size, structure, and posture its military forces. To size and shape its military forces, DoD needs a reasonably coherent defense planning methodology. Unless its choices concerning the size, composition, and capabilities of its military forces, including its army, are entirely political or arbitrary, DoD must develop some rational mechanism for generating requirements. How many ground forces (and air, sea, space, cyber, and other capabilities) are appropriate for supporting the nation's defense strategy, and why? This is the burden of *defense planning*—the employment of analytical, planning, and programming efforts to determine what sort of armed forces a state needs.

Today, DoD faces challenges in conducting defense planning. Traditionally, the Office of the Secretary of Defense (OSD) identifies its defense strategy and then selects scenarios that reflect the central elements of the chosen defense strategy and the operating environment envisaged by the leadership of the department. The results of the analysis of the scenarios inform OSD on the size and mix of forces and capabilities called for to implement the chosen defense strategy within expected fiscal limits. However, given today's dynamic and unpredictable security environment, the defense planning process should be broadened to consider a wider range of scenarios that reflect a wider range of potential geostrategic environments and alternative demands on U.S. military forces.

The current defense planning processes tend to base decisions on mostly inflexible assumptions and, as a result, introduce increased risk in those decisions if the assumptions turn out to be wrong. The force-sizing scenarios also do not account for uncertainty—the potential for many possible futures to emerge and the inability of any planning process to accurately identify the range of scenarios that might place the dominant demands on the force in 10 years or 20 years. This mismatch between current planning processes and the emerging strategic environment—such as the slow response to changing conditions in Europe, with potentially very large implications for allied ground forces—has been especially challenging for the U.S. Army.

Given this, both the Army and the wider DoD could benefit from new, broader approaches to force planning that could address these challenges. This report is the second part of a three-phase project that addresses those challenges.

What Are the Typical Approaches to Defense Planning?

As shown in Figure S.1, approaches to defense planning fall into two main categories, further divided into three subcategories. All of these approaches begin with national-level strategic guidance: the National Security Strategy (NSS), the National Defense Strategy (NDS), and the National Military Strategy (NMS).

At the broadest level, the starting point for a defense planning methodology can be either demand- or supply-based. The majority of defense planning activities tend to be demand-based, meaning that strategies, capabilities, and capacities are based on ideas about the requirements of potential future engagements. These demands can be derived from either threats or desired capabilities, or some combination of the two. It is a top-down planning method that begins with high-level strategic demand signals from which it derives requirements.

On the other hand, supply-based planning begins with a specific real-world constraint, such as current force size, capabilities mix, or budget limits, and builds forces from that baseline. It is more of a bottom-up planning method that starts with a base of existing capabilities and a presumed resource constraint and builds upward, making tweaks or incremental planned changes to the current force.

In both demand- and supply-based planning approaches, policymakers develop requirements, assess capabilities and capacity, account for constraints, and incorporate risk. However, the relative emphasis placed on each of these components varies between approaches, and such emphases can have particular advantages and disadvantages. The ultimate goal of the process is a feasible and affordable capabilities mix and,

Figure S.1
Overview of Defense Planning Approaches

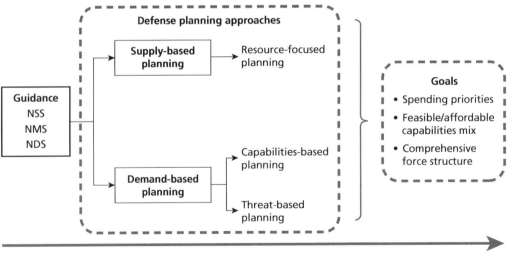

Process of translating guidance into force structure

ultimately, a comprehensive force structure that meets the demands of the strategy and the operating environment. These types of planning are reflected in Figure S.1.

Our analysis shows that each defense planning approach has advantages and disadvantages. In practice, any defense planning approach must take elements from both a demand-based and a resource-focused approach and include a discussion of both threats and capabilities. While the initial development of strategy requires a focus on desired outcomes, implementation must be grounded in realism about the capabilities and nature of the existing forces and about feasibility and affordability. An implementation plan, once devised, must again be assessed against its ability to achieve the desired outcomes. If a gap exists between the results of the top-down and bottom-up processes, this, at least theoretically, captures some notion of the risk that planners knowingly accept; the resource-driven force is less capable than what was prescribed by the top-down approach in some way, leading to risk. The challenge in successful defense planning lies in assessing capabilities, capacity, and risk using a blended planning approach. No matter what the starting point for planning, the methods that assess a proposed future force's performance in a variety of future scenarios are what ultimately provide valuable information to decisionmakers.

Challenges in Defense Planning Methodology: The Use of Scenarios

Overall, we find that the basic structure and approach of the force planning process can be effective in achieving its overarching goals. The existing process gives senior leaders an opportunity to test specific proposed force designs against detailed contingencies. It creates an ongoing dialogue about the contingencies that could plausibly call for U.S. military responses. And increasingly over the past year, more-responsive wargaming techniques have become more common. The process is not "broken," in other words, and generates significant insight that can contribute to senior leadership judgment about force design.

Yet, the process still suffers from two notable flaws that constrain its effectiveness. First, despite recent changes, it is still not responsive enough to quickly adapt to changes in the strategic environment and offer robust but quick-turn findings on the demands of newly arising contingencies. This problem may become even more worrisome as we enter a period of significant global turbulence, where the set of most plausible or most concerning scenarios could shift quickly. Second, the process tends to narrow on singular "approved solutions" that arbitrarily constrain the consideration of alternative forms contingencies might take or distinct operating concepts the United States might adopt in dealing with them.

Recommendations

Our recommendations are largely oriented around the challenges identified and around the findings presented above. The primary recommendations are shown in Table S.1.

Based on the results of this study, a major theme that will be brought over into the Phase Three substantive analysis is one of change and evolution. An additional or renewed framework for defense planning can profitably focus on areas of change in the major scenarios, thus providing additional insight on the responsiveness required in defense planning.

Table S.1
Proposed Recommendations

Recommendation	Characteristics of Recommendation
Explore a broader set of low-fidelity scenarios to hedge against surprise	Use a "scenario skunkworks" that constantly generates scenarios, contingencies, alternative concepts of operations (CONOPS), key assumptions, or other distinct ways of defining and approaching problems for in-depth assessment and then offers them as candidates for possible comprehensive treatment; this team could serve as scouts exploring the geostrategic horizon.
Explore current scenarios with a focus on innovation	Bring joint, cross-functional teams to bear on crucial operational dilemmas, focusing on underappreciated opportunities to achieve the NSS's policy goals.
Anticipate disruption; prioritize beyond the force-sizing construct	Have the planning process highlight three or four scenarios that senior leaders agree are the most useful to join the top-tier list of day-to-day benchmarking scenarios; discuss and debate these scenarios in terms of the various forms they could take, the CONOPS that the United States could choose to deal with them, and the potential force requirements; these would be initial, rough-cut looks that would streamline the process of more-complete examination if and when senior leaders made that determination.
Assess the impact of critical assumptions and choices	Take more seriously the need to identify key assumptions built into each scenario and subject assumptions to rigorous analysis and debate. Doing so would inform the discussion with a clearer understanding of the relationship between specific assumptions and outcomes.

Acknowledgments

The authors wish to acknowledge our sponsors and other contacts within the U.S. Department of Defense for providing data and expertise. We would also like to thank several experts at RAND, including Jim Cahill, Michael Johnson, Igor Mikolic-Torreira, David Ochmanek, Sally Sleeper, and Peter Wilson, for their inputs and comments on various drafts. We would also like to thank Ochmanek and Christine Wormuth for extensive and extremely helpful peer-review comments on an earlier draft. Any errors of fact or interpretation are the authors' alone.

Abbreviations

CAPE	Cost Assessment and Program Evaluation
CJCS	Chairman of the Joint Chiefs of Staff
COA	course of action
COCOM	combatant command
CONOPS	concepts of operations
CONPLAN	concept plan
DoD	U.S. Department of Defense
DPG	Defense Planning Guidance
DPS	Defense Planning Scenario
FYDP	Future Years Defense Program
GAO	U.S. Government Accountability Office
ISC	integrated security construct
ISIS	Islamic State in Iraq and Syria
MCO	major combat operation
NDS	National Defense Strategy
NMS	National Military Strategy
NSS	National Security Strategy
OMB	Office of Management and Budget
OPLAN	operational plan

OSD   Office of the Secretary of Defense

OUSD(Policy)   Office of the Undersecretary of Defense for Policy

POM   Program Objective Memorandum

PPBES   Planning, Programming, Budgeting, and Execution System

QDR   Quadrennial Defense Review

SME   subject-matter expert

SSA   support for strategic analysis

CHAPTER ONE

Introduction

Background

The Burden of Defense Planning

The U.S. Department of Defense (DoD) relies on planning processes to size, structure, and posture its military forces. To size and shape its military forces, DoD needs a reasonably coherent defense planning methodology. Unless its choices concerning the size, composition, and capabilities of its military forces, including its army, are entirely political or arbitrary, it must develop some rational mechanism for generating requirements. How many and what types of forces (and ground, air, sea, space, cyber, and other capabilities) are called for, and why? This is the burden of *defense planning*—the employment of analytical, planning, and programming efforts to determine what sort of armed forces are appropriate for a state.

The following question has been a perennial one in modern defense debates: What size and composition of force would best equip the Joint Force and, in particular, the U.S. Army to meet the set of demands presented by the security environment and the mission set outlined in defense strategy documents? During the Cold War, the question was answered largely in terms of the pacing threat of the Soviet Union. Without the lodestone of the Soviet Union, during the 1990s, the planning context became more diverse and complex with a wider range of threats and missions. But the challenge for defense planning remained the same—to look across the spectrum of threats, opportunities, demands, and missions and design a force best equipped to promote the nation's interests.

States can make such judgments based on a number of potential criteria. They can plan their forces against specific threats, judging their needs by the operational requirements of fighting a specific potential enemy (or set of them). They can identify broad capabilities deemed necessary to support the state's national security strategy. No matter what approach they take, defense planners will be forced to consider constraints on resources at some point: All defense planning will be resource-*informed*, operating under the constraint of a range of plausible national security funding levels. Some can be very explicitly resource-*directed*, using a hypothetical top-line as a principal constraint for shaping the force.

Defense planning processes represent an attempt to introduce a rational and objective mechanism for deriving force requirements from a very complex and messy national security context. However, one of the leading themes of defense planning is that while it is intended to be objective, the result will always retain a strong degree of imprecision. Many links along the analytical chain involve significant degrees of guesswork, major assumptions, or choices that reflect expert judgment. However, they have also shown remarkable durability over time—a result of largely bipartisan consensus over many critical (though analytically intractable) defense planning assumptions, and path dependencies resulting from the bureaucratic institutionalization of past choices. This then becomes a dominant question for defense planning processes: By what objective standard can the leaders of the U.S. defense enterprise be confident that the force they choose is best aligned with U.S. strategy and policy goals?

That question implies something that is equally important—understanding the sources of variability in defense planning outcomes. In scenario-based planning, aligning forces with strategy entails both the selection of scenarios as a basis for quantifying demand and then the development of a Joint Force that can meet that demand. Different assumptions and types of guidance can produce very different results in the process, but these outcomes are not always apparent to senior defense leaders who are not engaged in the day-to-day planning effort. It is important to understand the most powerful sources of variability. If one especially powerful assumption is responsible for one-third of the requirements estimate for a given force element, for example, and the results prove insensitive to painstaking changes to the modeling, the more important discussions might be about whether the assumption is necessary (and not tweaks to capabilities that affect the modeling result).

The Challenge of Defense Planning Today

Currently, DoD faces challenges in conducting defense planning. Traditionally, the Office of the Secretary of Defense (OSD) identifies its defense strategy and investment priorities. OSD then selects scenarios that reflect the central elements of the anticipated security environment, the chosen defense strategy, and office priorities. The results of the analysis of the selected scenarios inform OSD on the size and mix of forces and capabilities called for to implement the chosen defense strategy within expected fiscal limits.

However, given the dynamic and unpredictable security environment, we find that the defense planning process should be broadened to consider a wider set of scenarios that reflect a greater range of potential geostrategic environments and/or the resulting U.S. defense strategy. The existing processes for defense planning tend to base decisions on largely inflexible assumptions and introduce increased risk in those decisions. This risk is evident from the most recent force-sizing efforts, which did not address now-known threats, including Russia and the Islamic State in Iraq and Syria (ISIS). Force-sizing scenarios also did not adequately account for uncertainty—the potential for many possible futures to emerge and the inability of any planning process to accurately identify the range of scenarios that might place the dominant demands on the force 10 years or 20 years hence.

This mismatch between current planning processes and the emerging strategic environment is especially challenging for the Army. The current defense strategy emphasizes relying on air power and sea power and takes risk in ground forces, especially those that may be needed for a second major combat operation (MCO) or for large, long-duration stability operations. The defense strategy relies on the Army's ability to regenerate forces rapidly to address potential capacity shortfalls, although recent experience suggests that regeneration of sizable forces would take years, not weeks or months. But the current roster of approved planning scenarios remains small in number and may not capture the full range of contingencies that could confront the U.S. military.

Given this, both the Army and the wider DoD could benefit from new, broader approaches to force planning that could address at least two core issues: (1) the requirements of planning for some degree of uncertainty, rather than for a finite and traditional set of scenarios; and (2) the range of additional scenarios that would adequately represent both expected/likely and possible operational demands for U.S. military forces.

Objectives

This report is part of a three-phase project.[1] The Phase One report provided a description of the factors that shaped conventional ground force planning over the 1945–2015 period, with an emphasis on the strategic concepts and contingency scenarios used and the identification of broader lessons of likely interest to contemporary force planners. This second report focuses specifically on the strategic concepts that help to connect basic national security policies to the planning and development of conventional ground forces. It also provides context for the consideration of different combinations of alternative force planning scenarios. The third phase study will turn to a substantive analysis of the Army that the nation needs, offering a framework for evaluating the current scenario set in ways that provide insight on current Army choices and trade-offs.

This report on Phase Two offers an overview of DoD's current defense planning process. For this study, the term *defense planning* is synonymous with the more-specific discipline of force planning. It refers to procedural mechanisms by which DoD translates guidance in the National Security Strategy (NSS)—the interests, objectives, and norms to be promoted and defended and assessments of the present and future threats

---

[1] Eric V. Larson, *Force Planning Scenarios, 1945–2016: Their Origins and Use in Defense Strategic Planning*, Santa Monica, Calif.: RAND Corporation, RR-2173-A, forthcoming.

and challenges in the strategic environment—into decisions on the size, composition, and posture of future military forces. Therefore, for this report, *defense planning* refers both to the analytical methods used to make this connection as well as the institutional processes established within DoD (and the services) to accomplish it.

This report focuses on the use of scenarios—specific potential contingencies against which forces can be sized and designed and capabilities developed—because of their long-standing role in defense planning processes. Scenarios, it is important to emphasize, do more than provide a benchmark against which planners can estimate how much the U.S. military will need to fight a certain contingency. Ideally, scenarios become part of the discussion in defense planning at the intersection of many factors—operational requirements, readiness and posture issues, available resources, alternative operational concepts, legal and political constraints on operations, and more. Scenarios can help illustrate how the U.S. military will fight, given resource constraints: Given what the United states will have, what is it able to do and how best can it accomplish its goals? Properly employed, scenarios contribute to many aspects of defense planning—discussions about the size, design, cost, and risk of the force.

Approach and Scope

To accomplish this phase's objective, we used several means of gathering data and reaching conclusions. Because this subject has a limited extant literature, the first and, ultimately primary, approach was a series of structured dialogues with current and former participants in the defense planning process. We reviewed existing studies where they were available and surveyed the limited number of official documents that discuss elements of the defense planning process. We catalogued the leading defense planning processes in some detail, checking the understanding of RAND experts with current participants in the process. We held a number of sessions among RAND subject-matter experts (SMEs) with personal experience in the defense planning process to elicit lessons from their experience. We also relied heavily on the background and findings of the Phase One study mentioned earlier, which surveyed the history of scenario-based defense planning and provided a detailed understanding of the strengths and weaknesses of various approaches over time.

From a scoping perspective, this study is a relatively modest effort that does not build a new planning process from the ground up. Instead, it concentrates on outlining the criteria for a more-effective approach and identifying and describing a number of additional scenarios that could be used to appropriately broaden defense planning.

Also, the findings and recommendations reflect what must be understood as a qualitative expert judgment. There is no way to generate an objective, quantitative finding as to the "best" or optimal form of defense planning. There are too many variables and goals involved; defense leaders want too many different things from the process for an easy optimization function, and debates over planning are often about one value versus another (rather than any particular output). To reach our judgments, we have sought the best current information available about the process, and we gathered the best insight we could discover about its strengths and weaknesses and areas for improvement.

Organization of This Report

As context, Chapter Two begins by establishing terminology that allows us to distinguish between various approaches to defense planning. Chapter Three provides our key findings, focusing on how scenarios are used to inform defense planning and then citing some general challenges with the use of scenarios. Chapter Four concludes with a number of recommendations for improving the use of scenarios in defense planning.

CHAPTER TWO

What Are the Typical Approaches to Defense Planning?

Introduction

As defined in this study in Chapter One, the primary goal of defense planning is to translate the NSS and derivative defense strategies and guidance documents—including the National Defense Strategy (NDS), the National Military Strategy (NMS), and the Defense Planning Guidance (DPG)—into a set of spending priorities, a feasible and affordable capabilities mix, and, ultimately, a comprehensive force structure. While the NSS and NDS establish strategic goals based on U.S. interests, these overarching statements are not granular or specific enough to directly link to military objectives and strategies. DoD generally uses some scenario-based method to link broad strategic goals to a concrete funding scheme that provides capabilities appropriate to execute the missions called for by the strategies. However, a variety of subtle differences in the foundation and framework for this method can affect execution.

This chapter lays out the two approaches to defense planning and then defines and describes three categories within those two approaches (as shown in Figure 2.1), all of which begin with national-level strategic guidance—the NSS, NDS, and the NMS. At a high level, the starting point for a defense planning methodology can be either demand- or supply-based. The majority of current defense planning work, at least at the strategic level, is demand-based planning, meaning that strategies, capabilities, and capacities are based on ideas about the requirements of potential future engagements. In particular, within supply-based planning, the later analysis in this chapter will focus on one category—resource-focused planning, which begins with a specific real-world constraint, such as current force size, capabilities mix, or budget limits.

In both demand- and supply-based (or resource-focused) planning approaches, policymakers develop requirements, assess capabilities and capacity, account for constraints, and incorporate risk. But the relative emphasis placed on each of these components varies between approaches, and such emphases can have particular advantages and disadvantages. The ultimate goal of the process is, as shown in Figure 2.1, spending priorities, a feasible or affordable capabilities mix, and, ultimately, a comprehensive force structure. To achieve a balanced approach to force planning, using both of these

Figure 2.1
Overview of Defense Planning Approaches

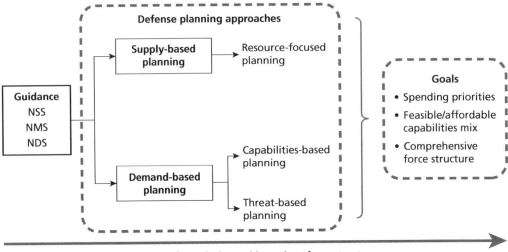

Process of translating guidance into force structure

RAND *RR2173/2-2.1*

approaches at different stages can bring a variety of insights to the defense planning process.

Defense planning is also an exercise in communication. U.S. force structure decisions, and the messages broadcast during the force planning process that take place around them, tell U.S. and international audiences about the U.S. view of the nature of the worldwide security environment, U.S. intentions and capabilities, and the U.S. commitment to sustaining promises. Within DoD, elements of the defense planning process also represent efforts by OSD to communicate to the services and vice versa. Thus, defense planning has multiple goals, some analytical and some public. The choice of scenarios is not merely an objective analytical function; in practice, it also sends messages about the major tasks that the United States is preparing to undertake.

As mentioned briefly in Chapter One, the dominant challenge to analytical rigor in defense planning is that just about every major step or transition in the process contains elements of uncertainty. From the beginning, the choice of scenarios involves applying judgment and approximation, based on the current strategic context, as much as it represents an analytical exercise in anticipating future conflict. The definition of success in each contingency can be altered and, in any case, may allow significant room for interpretation. For example, although many of the scenarios have remained constant over time in terms of the adversary, the nature of the contingency, the Joint Force's objectives, and the assumptions have evolved.[1] The choice of an operating concept to handle a specific scenario significantly influences the amount and type of forces

---

[1]   Discussions with current and former DoD officials.

required. One result is that the process has a significant risk of false precision, particularly as the analysis encompasses detailed modeling that seems to "prove" how the war fight will play out: Defense planning processes often generate seemingly precise, quantified outcomes that give an unrealistic sense of the accuracy of the efforts. Those involved in the process are generally well aware of these challenges, but a continuing challenge of defense planning is how to handle the inevitable uncertainty and ambiguity involved in such estimates.

The process also inevitably involves a degree of bureaucratic influence. A typical assumption in evaluating the effectiveness of defense planning is that civilian defense leaders are looking for options—outcomes to be had at variable levels of effort—while military planners are looking for clear guidance about objectives and missions. In fact, both sides are seeking autonomy. The military is seeking autonomy over ways and means, under a theory of civil-military relations that views the civilian contribution to strategy development as limited, largely to the specification of political ends. Civilians are seeking autonomy from military efforts to constrain policymakers to their preferred strategies, where *strategy* is understood as an alignment of ends, ways, and means.

The saving grace of this process is that all the parties are authentically interested in advancing national security. Each side simply views it through different lenses, creating a diversity of strategic options for policymakers—if those policymakers have the bandwidth and expertise to investigate the available options. The problem is not so much the differing views of the two sides or the fact that there are differences, as much as the fact that the scenario development process, as practiced by DoD today, is so inflexible, costly, and time-consuming that policymakers are boxed into making choices within an unnecessarily narrow set of boundaries.

In the remainder of this chapter, we discuss the planning approaches shown in Figure 2.1, as well as the advantages and disadvantages of those approaches. We also discuss the use of scenarios in demand-based planning approaches, as well as their advantages and disadvantages. Finally, we discuss how defense planning is actually done today, examine the need to incorporate risk into defense planning, and suggest various hedging or alternative futures approaches that can achieve this goal.

Demand-Based Planning Approaches

Throughout modern history, DoD has generally chosen demand-based methodologies as a starting point for defense planning. Demand-based methodologies involve deriving requirements from broad national objectives: The methodologies focus on a desired set of capabilities, outcomes, and missions as a basis for defense planning. The desired "ends" for what a future force can achieve provide the foundation for this type of planning. As we will see, these ends can come from a number of sources, including threats produced by specific potential adversaries and the capability requirements of generic missions. Either way, demand-based approaches are thus a natural extension of an application of the NDS. Any defense planning process must involve some degree of demand-based analysis to ensure that outcomes are connected to the higher-level national strategies.

Demand-based methodologies focus on what the decisionmaker wants to accomplish, centering planning efforts on the size and characteristics of potential future conflicts. Recent demand-based planning efforts have been rooted in some variant of the classic "two-war" force planning criterion. Since at least the 1960s, as outlined in the Phase One report,[2] the U.S. military has measured its requirements against a posited number of conflicts to help size and structure the force. As the United States has global responsibilities and potential adversaries in multiple regions, force planning must account for the possibility that one or more adversaries could act opportunistically when the United States finds itself in a conflict in a different part of the world. U.S. forces must be sized and structured to fight more than one major conflict in a given time frame. The "defeat/deny" concept of the 2014 Quadrennial Defense Review (QDR) represents the current variant of this two-war construct, stating that the U.S. military will be able to simultaneously

- defend the homeland
- conduct sustained, distributed counterterrorist operations
- deter aggression and assure allies in multiple regions through forward-presence and engagement.

If deterrence fails,

- U.S. forces will be capable of defeating a regional adversary in a large-scale, multiphase campaign.
- U.S. forces will be capable of denying the objectives of—or imposing unacceptable costs on—a second aggressor in another region.[3]

In addition to the posited number of conflicts, demand-based planning methodologies tend to look to a number of variables or factors to evaluate threats and needed capabilities, including

- mission and objectives
- adversary capabilities, objectives, and behaviors

---

[2]   Larson, forthcoming.

[3]   There is some debate about whether "defeat/deny" constitutes a true two-war force-sizing construct. We do not address that debate here, but only note that the architects of the doctrine intended for it to reflect the ability of the United States to deal with more than one major conflict simultaneously. See DoD, *Quadrennial Defense Review 2014*, Washington, D.C., March 2014.

- ally and partner capabilities and contributions
- types of conflicts (e.g., large-scale combined-arms, air/maritime, irregular warfare)
- geographic location of conflicts
- U.S. access rights and assumptions in different potential conflict regions
- frequency, timing, and duration of conflicts
- warning, ability to control timing of conflict, and associated readiness issues.

Advantages of Demand-Based Planning Approaches

Given this, demand-based approaches reflect an effort to derive very specific requirements from very broad objectives. As such, these approaches in general share a number of advantages. These approaches fit well into the larger national defense planning methodology. Strategic goals articulated in the NSS, such as the ability to conduct specific types of missions, can directly form the basis of a demand-based approach. They encourage a focus on high-level requirements and a thorough survey of future needs likely to identify gaps. And they establish a coherent high-level strategy early in the planning process.

This broad guidance provides a useful template for evaluating more-granular prioritization, investment, and strategy decisions. As an example, one possible demand-based planning construct could emphasize a dominant focus on a pacing threat of major regional conflict and judge investment decisions primarily against that.

Disadvantages of Demand-Based Planning Approaches

Such approaches can also carry some disadvantages. If not implemented correctly, demand-based planning approaches can ignore budgetary, technology, and timing constraints for too long in the planning process, focusing on high-level strategic goals unconstrained by resource concerns. Also, without an early focus on realistic constraints, demand-based planning can produce impractical results. Such approaches can lose sight of the challenges and cost of transitioning from today's military and capabilities to a desired future state. Laying out the "demand" to conduct certain force projection missions could delay a recognition that such missions might be becoming cost-prohibitive. And they can focus on a single strategy or concept too early in the planning process. While a specific strategic objective could be achieved in many different ways, demand-based planning tends to focus in on a specific approach, plan, or set of scenarios, the result of which is limited opportunity to question assumptions later in the process.

As shown in Figure 2.1, demand-based approaches are sometimes grouped into two categories: *threat-based* and *capabilities-based*. We discuss each below, along with their advantages and disadvantages.

Threat-Based Approaches

Threat-based planning approaches are rooted in specific potential future adversaries and conflicts. These specific conflicts are then used to develop force structure and posture plans. Such approaches describe goals in terms of the ability to counter a specific current or future threat, as described in the high-level strategy documents that serve as the basis for planning in this model. Traditionally, threat-based methodologies have been most popular when the set of potential adversaries and the threats they pose are well agreed upon within the U.S. national security community. For example, threat-based planning was commonly used by DoD throughout the Cold War era.[4] During this time, planners felt they could identify the *largest* potential threat facing the nation. Planning against this threat would then also allow the United States to face other potential conflicts ("lesser and included" cases).

Threat-based planning constructs are driven by U.S. objectives, opponent capabilities, and forces required to counter these capabilities. This includes not only *actual* differences in capabilities between the United States and its adversaries but also *perceived* differences or gaps that may affect foreign relations and the ability to deter future conflicts.

In the current context, a widely discussed example of threat-based planning is the Korea contingency. The U.S. commitment to support its ally, South Korea, and implement policies to deter military aggression and provocations by North Korea appear as prominent objectives in all recent U.S. national security strategies and defense planning documents. A threat-based planning approach evaluates the specific capabilities held by North Korea and develops requirements for U.S. force size and composition based on the need to achieve U.S. goals in the face of those specific adversary capabilities. North Korean efforts to develop powerful asymmetric warfare capabilities in the form of extensive special operating forces, for example, would create a demand for U.S. and allied responses: base and port defense, coastal surveillance, an effective Integrated Air Defense System to prevent airborne infiltration, and so on. The required U.S. capabilities are a function of the demands created by U.S. and allied objectives and enemy strengths.

Advantages of Threat-Based Planning

Like demand-based defense planning in general, threat-based planning has a number of advantages:

- It encourages a detailed and rigorous focus on the adversary, so that U.S. capabilities do not become untethered from the actual military forces it will fight. In

---

[4]   John F. Troxell, *Force Planning in an Era of Uncertainty: Two MRCs as a Force Sizing Framework*, Carlisle Barracks, Pa.: Strategic Studies Institute, U.S. Army War College, September 15, 1997, p. 2; regarding the debate between former Chairman of the Joint Chiefs of Staff (CJCS) GEN Colin L. Powell and former Secretary of Defense Les Aspin on capability- and threat-based planning, see pp. 10–12.

broad terms, U.S. defense planning decisions should reflect a close awareness of potential adversary capabilities and of the concepts and doctrines by which U.S. forces intend to defeat them.

- It can be successful at many levels, from assessing overall military strength in relation to an adversary to comparing vulnerabilities in a specific capability area during a particular future scenario.
- It provides an opportunity to focus investments on equipment and capabilities in those areas that are critical for the most-significant potential future conflicts, when those threats can be agreed upon by all stakeholders. This can reduce costs associated with focusing on risk and a large number of future scenarios.
- It includes a wide variety of potential future threats in the assessment portion of the defense planning effort, which can allow planners to incorporate uncertainty.
- It provides the opportunity to include the unique political landscape surrounding potential future real-world conflicts, allowing for the inclusion of diplomatic relations with specific countries and their allies throughout the planning process.
- It becomes an ancillary benefit for those familiar with the operational dilemmas that forces may face in the future (President Dwight Eisenhower's "plans are useless, but planning is indispensable").
- It provides a compelling basis for explaining the resulting decisions regarding the shape of the future force and the resources required to support it, as these are predicated on the demands of deterring and defeating real adversaries.

Disadvantages of Threat-Based Planning

These approaches also have distinct limitations and risks. Many of them flow from the uncertainties and ambiguities inherent in the process of generating defense requirements from a set of demands, threats, and missions—the specifics of which cannot be fully foreseen:

- These approaches require a certain level of agreement on the appropriate set of adversaries, as well as the ability to attain detailed information on their capabilities and intentions. Future threats and information on current/future capabilities are always uncertain. Thus, finding the necessary agreement on likely future threats while developing an assessment methodology that still incorporates uncertainty is challenging.
- They can lead to a reactive planning culture because of the need to establish an agreed-upon set of relevant future threats. Planners focus on understanding a particular future conflict and gathering information on a specific adversary's capabilities, often predicated on recent experience and current threat perceptions, thus running the risk of losing sight of other potential threats.
- Given strong agreement about future conflicts, they can overemphasize a single threat-specific concept or capability without sufficient analysis of the utility of that capability with regard to the overall national strategy.

- They tend to focus on contingency operations, particularly the warfighting phases of a conflict, at the expense of peacetime and postconflict needs. Care must be taken in the assessment portion of the planning process to ensure that demand is understood and capabilities and capacity are assessed across the full mission set and all phases of potential future conflicts.

Capabilities-Based Planning Approaches

Within the broad category of demand-based defense planning, the main theoretical alternative to threat-based planning is capabilities-based planning, as shown in Figure 2.1. Capabilities-based planning focuses less on identifying specific adversaries and more on analyzing the types of capabilities likely to be needed in a set of less–well-defined possible future wars. Specifically, this set of methods is based on a desired set of capabilities that the armed forces should possess to counter a more-vaguely defined future threat or meet a strategy-based set of generic future objectives. Instead of using specific likely future threats as the foundation for defense planning, capabilities-based planning broadly assesses the types of capabilities the military will need against an array of future conflicts. The goal of this method is to allow for the development of planning constructs even when there is not strong agreement on current or future opponent capabilities.[5] Proponents of capabilities-based planning hope that such an approach would reduce the need to force a complicated, uncertain future world into an overly stylized set of planning constructs. The problem, of course, is that it is difficult to think meaningfully about prospective conflicts absent a sense of whom one might be fighting, over what stakes, under what conditions, and with what forces.

Needed capabilities are sometimes defined in terms of either *objectives* or *missions*. Objective-based planning focuses on the *goals* a future force should be able to achieve.[6] Examples of possible objectives include providing humanitarian aid, deterring a major opponent, or fighting multiple regional conflicts. Mission-based planning defines the set of required capabilities by choosing *critical wartime missions* that a future force will need to accomplish.[7] Examples of such missions include strategic surveillance, force

---

[5]   Paul K. Davis recommends this approach, and he has argued that the process "was too often rigid, unrealistic, monolithic, and stereotyped" (see Paul K. Davis, ed., *New Challenges for Defense Planning: Rethinking How Much Is Enough*, Santa Monica, Calif.: RAND Corporation, MG-400-RC, 1994, p. 5; and Paul K. Davis and Lou Finch, *Defense Planning for the Post–Cold War Era: Giving Meaning to Flexibility, Adaptiveness, and Robustness of Capability*, Santa Monica, Calif.: RAND Corporation, MR-322-JS, 1993, p. xxii.

[6]   See, for example, Glenn A. Kent and William E. Simons, "Objective-Based Planning," in Paul K. Davis, ed., *New Challenges for Defense Planning: Rethinking How Much Is Enough*, Santa Monica, Calif.: RAND Corporation, MR-400-RC, 1994, pp. 59–71. As the chapter makes clear, the objectives can be either very broad and strategic or very discrete and operational.

[7]   Richard L. Kugler makes a case for mission-based planning against a generic set of contingencies in Richard L. Kugler, "Nonstandard Contingencies for Defense Planning," in Paul K. Davis, ed., *New Challenges for Defense*

protection, or movement. While not explicitly focused on objectives, the set of missions to be accomplished is ideally informed by assumptions about future objectives. Therefore, the line between objective-based and mission-based planning is not always clear—there is a significant degree of overlap between the two approaches.

Advantages of Capabilities-Based Planning

Like threat-based planning, a capabilities-based approach has a number of advantages:

- It does not require comprehensive agreement on the set of future adversaries and their capabilities nor identifying specific states as potential enemies, thus potentially easing the risk of an overly narrow focus for force planning.
- It can lead to a more forward-looking culture and less-reactive approaches to force planning, given the lack of an agreed-upon set of future conflicts.
- It may help identify capability gaps that are difficult to conceive when considering only real-world threat-based scenarios, given some level of abstraction, including the removal of real-world politics and diplomacy.

Disadvantages of Capabilities-Based Planning

There are also some disadvantages to this approach:

- It can be far removed from future threats and potential missions in its pure or extreme form. It may be difficult to understand the types of capabilities required without implicitly enumerating threats we are likely to face, which can, in turn, also reduce the perceived value or meaning of the resulting findings.
- It does not naturally and immediately incorporate detailed operational planning, including sustainment, timing, operational concepts, and posture, because such planning does not focus on a specific future conflict. As such, its more-generic approach to outlining threats can miss specific emerging capabilities in the hands of a particular potential adversary.
- It is inherently weak in the face of entrenched institutional priorities, possibly leading to requirements growth. Because the demand for capabilities does not have to be directly linked to a future threat or conflict, it becomes easier for stakeholders to point to desirable capabilities that defend current force structure or other institutional predilections.
- It can inadvertently remove political concerns from the planning process. Such concerns as strategic partnerships, ally reactions, and potential for escalation may be underemphasized when capabilities are removed from the real-world environments in which they could be needed. A planning approach that focuses exclusively on concepts of operations (CONOPS) for achieving a particular goal could

---

Planning: Rethinking How Much Is Enough, Santa Monica, Calif.: RAND Corporation, MR-400-RC, 1994, pp. 192–195.

miss important contextual issues, such as the effects of a certain course of action on global politics or the risk of escalation when plans are executed against a real-world enemy. While abstraction can lead to more creative thinking, it may produce results that are not practical, feasible, or credible against actual adversaries.

- Unless some kind of stratification and prioritization strategy is used, it can lead to an overwhelming level of effort to effectively execute such planning, while still creating the depth and granularity of planning factors required for force planning.
- It lacks cogency as a basis for explaining the choices made in constructing the force and the need for resources to field it.
- It can prove more difficult to gain acceptance as a basis for planning, since process stakeholders and senior decisionmakers may see abstract problems and notional adversaries as less plausible or tractable to support real-world choices.

The Use of Scenarios in Demand-Based Planning

Demand-based planning—be it threat-based or capabilities-based—relies heavily on the use of scenarios to provide a concrete context for planning discussions. Planning for specific threats uses scenarios to assess capacity and make tradeoffs between capabilities. Although scenarios vary in their purpose, level of detail, link to real-world circumstances, and many other characteristics, they aim to provide a concrete example to serve as a basis for evaluating the capacity and capabilities of the force.

In the process, scenarios can serve a number of useful purposes. They create tangible challenges against which to measure capabilities and allow U.S. defense planners to conduct these tests. Scenarios are one of the most useful tools for moving abstract discussions on future needs to a more-grounded analysis that forces planners to address such parameters as the nature and size of the threat, terrain, operational concepts, timing and warning, posture, and deployability.[8] Scenarios can place potential adversary capabilities in a specific context and create detailed contingencies, which can be used to guide the development of defense requirements.

Recognizing these possible values, DoD today extensively uses scenarios in the development of its plans and programs. Scenarios and integrated scenario sets are a leading touchstone for measuring the needs and sufficiency of the defense posture. This section lays out some general benefits and pitfalls of scenario usage, while Chapter Three offers a more in-depth analysis of the challenges of the current process of scenario development and application.

To benefit from the advantages and mitigate the disadvantages of both threat-based and capabilities-based planning, there is a need to carefully develop a scenario-

---

[8]   Troxell, 1997, p. 19.

based assessment mechanism. While threat-based planning lends itself most easily to developing good scenarios, such planning must be careful to avoid too narrow a focus on a small set of specific future conflicts. While capabilities-based planning hopes to avoid focus on a specific set of future adversaries, it may be difficult to develop credible scenarios that reflect the desired set of future capabilities. No matter which type of defense planning methodology scenarios are supporting, their use has advantages and disadvantages.

Advantages of Scenarios in Demand-Based Planning

- These scenarios provide a specific and detailed focus for defense planning that can provide the necessary environment for effective decisionmaking. They offer precise situations and threats against which to judge the capabilities and capacity of one or more forces.
- They may make it easier for planners to make difficult prioritization decisions, because detailed information on future needs helps identify the most-critical future capabilities. They also make the problem more "real" for participants because they can see a future where the posited scenario plays out, as opposed to a notional adversary or generic scenario.
- They provide a means for including a time element, thus forcing planners to consider both peak capacity and capabilities and readiness, sustainment, and CONOPS.

Disadvantages of Scenarios in Demand-Based Planning

- These scenarios exacerbate the risk of misidentifying future adversaries and their capabilities if used as single-point solutions or if a single or small number of scenarios is used to drive capability investments and force-sizing. The development of well-specified, detailed scenarios involves making many assumptions about not only who future adversaries are and what they are capable of but also the specific way in which a conflict is likely to unfold.
- They run the risk of becoming definitive when only meant to be illustrative. A planning process can show that the few scenarios used to generate requirements cover the entire universe of future demands, when, in fact, they are only representative examples. However, once dominated by scenarios, a planning process can easily fall into this trap, ignoring contingencies or requirements outside the assumed set. As explained later, it is possible to include variation, risk, and hedging even within a single scenario, but it can become difficult to develop the tools necessary for assessing a wide range of scenario modifications.
- They can be expensive and time-consuming to produce, especially the more-detailed scenarios that allow for improved planning. This is costly and can also

lead to a small number of scenarios being used as the basis for all planning efforts, given bandwidth limits.

- Given the expensive and time-consuming nature of scenario development, scenarios can cause a cultural reluctance to challenge assumptions or consider the investigation of alternative scenarios. The need for plausibility, buy-in from a variety of organizations at multiple levels, and careful vetting of assumptions can lead to a very slow development process.

Resource-Focused Planning Approaches

As shown in Figure 2.1, the other key planning approach is resource-focused planning, which represents a less-common alternative to the demand-based approaches discussed earlier and shown in the figure. Instead of emphasizing desired outcomes, a resource-focused planning approach focuses on identifying the best way ahead under today's constraints. Such approaches begin with the status quo and seek to identify the next set of changes that will lead to the development of a desirable future force. Oftentimes, the starting point for resource-focused planning is budget pressure or a tight fiscal environment. For this reason, resource-focused planning is also sometimes called *budget-driven planning*. It is a more zero-sum process than demand-based planning, which adds up potential requirements based on contingency analysis. Resource-focused planning considers available resources as a limit and looks at priorities, trade-offs, and substitution opportunities to meet the most possible potential demands from a finite resource base.

At first glance, this would seem to be an inappropriate and, perhaps, even dangerous approach to defense planning. Most major assessments of defense planning point to the need to make it a strategy-driven process—to begin with strategic objectives or ends and align the means, in this case, force structure and capabilities, to those ends.[9] Yet, part of the imprecision of the process is that many factors inevitably affect the outcome—the forces actually built—besides an objective assessment of their alignment to potential demands. Service culture and preferences, congressional views (sometimes related to the location of units or manufacturing locations for capabilities), and many other factors work together to help shape the Joint Force.

Resources are a dominant component of this mosaic of influences. No matter what a strategy calls for, if the nation will not apply the resources needed to fulfill it, strategy-based planning will fall short. Therefore, it may make some sense to start from the bottom up, with the resources the nation is likely to devote to the defense account, and conduct defense planning from that starting point. (It can also incorporate other

---

[9]   See, for example, Stephen Hadley and William Perry, *The QDR in Perspective: Meeting America's National Security Needs in the 21st Century—Final Report of the Quadrennial Defense Review Independent Panel*, Washington, D.C.: United States Institute of Peace, 2010.

constraints—service-based expectations about the shape of their forces, for example.) This approach can still incorporate strategy—it will shape the available resources based on strategy-inspired needs—but it begins with the likely supply and then seeks to modify it to best effect.

On a year-to-year basis, in fact, most Program Objective Memorandum (POM) development–related activity is resource-focused planning, even at the strategic level. Budget development, as a matter of bureaucratic practice, is an effort to maintain the planned program in the face of fact-of-life changes (e.g., inflation) and directed investments (e.g., third offset). On the strategic side, the set of integrated security constructs (ISCs) generated by the QDR process outlines several possible alternative "futures" in which the armed forces must operate. ISCs tend to be fairly stable over long periods. It is only when the international security environment is or budget constraints are particularly dynamic that scenario-based planning becomes an important driver of decisions.

Thus, every defense planning process incorporates elements of both demand- and resource-focused planning. In addition, as suggested above, scenarios can be an effective way of integrating the two approaches, by not only considering what is called for in a given contingency but also testing different concepts for how the United States could fight in various scenarios. Therefore, scenarios join a number of inputs to senior leadership dialogues that help generate the final defense judgments, which are inevitably the product of many intersecting factors.

Resource-focused planning is less focused on long-term strategy and represents a more-incremental approach to planning—looking for ways to modify a defense program on the margins but still in meaningful ways. While fiscal constraints and feasibility of developing a proposed future force from a current one must obviously inform all force defense planning, resource-focused planning puts these considerations at the forefront. The high degree of emphasis on the current force and today's constraints again has advantages and disadvantages.

Advantages of Resource-Focused Planning

- It is, by definition, grounded in reality and immediately addresses real-world constraints.
- It can encourage efforts to find creative solutions that stretch existing assets by its focus on constraints.
- It can be easier to translate into an implementation or transition plan, because such planning takes today's force as a starting point.

Disadvantages of Resource-Focused Planning

- It is difficult to incorporate long-term strategy and goals into this approach.

- It may fail to foresee and to adapt to future challenges, leading to capabilities gaps.
- It may focus too much on specific, immediate theater needs to fill small gaps, risking losing sight of a more global long-term strategy that may require short-term sacrifices.
- It may be difficult to reconcile a resource-focused strategy with high-level guidance, such as the NSS.

As imperfect as it may be, some form of resource-focused, budget-informed or bottom-up planning no doubt reflects to a significant degree how defense planning actually occurs. In part, this is true because there are so many layers of planning going on at the same time: Services do their own planning and then pass the results or recommendations on to OSD and ultimately the Secretary of Defense for an additional layer of judgment. Finally, it goes to the Office of Management and Budget (OMB) and the White House for determinations within the executive branch—and from there to Congress for the legislative layer. The result is far from a singular, objective defense planning process, and one implication is that participants sometimes begin making plans from the bottom up, knowing that guidance from the larger-scale top-down processes may be conflicting, somewhat vague, or not timely.

Defense Planning in Practice

While the taxonomy of defense planning shown in Figure 2.1 and discussed earlier is useful to understand the variety of theoretical defense planning approaches that could be applied, real-world distinctions between these methods are often less clear-cut than such a taxonomy suggests. There is a clear difference between the demand-based and resource-focused set of approaches, but a true application of a resource-focused method is rare outside of operational planning exercises. Among the demand-based methods, most realistic applications require a mixture of several approaches. While the distinction between threat-based and capabilities-based planning is commonly used, defense planning often occurs somewhere between these two approaches. In threat-based planning, expert judgment and analysis are used to identify the set of future threats against which to plan a force in an uncertain world. In capabilities-based planning, an understanding of likely real-world demands must inform the creation of a list of desired capabilities.

Thus, defense planning in practice tends to incorporate many different approaches to generate its outcomes. While demand- or resource-focused planning represent useful ideal types, actual planning efforts involve considerations from both of those and all their subtypes. If defense planning is to be relevant to decisionmakers, it must inevitably be resource-informed, for example, in addition to being demand-focused. Sometimes these influences happen informally, outside a structured planning process, such as when a senior leader might quickly discard a potential demand-based approach as unaffordable. Such a choice injects resource-focused thinking into the process, regardless of whether it is formally included.

One implication of this complexity of the planning process is that it becomes exceedingly difficult to find straightforward proposals for reform that can address the multiple goals, approaches, mindsets, and structures involved. *Defense planning is a resource-informed, politically influenced, strategically influenced effort, one in which generating optimal answers may well be impossible.* Offering recommendations for reform must take these complexities into account, especially in conceiving the specific purpose of the proposed change.

Risk and Uncertainty in Defense Planning

Regardless of which defense planning approach is used, we must recognize that defense planning is, unavoidably, a type of planning under uncertainty. There is uncertainty about which future fights the United States will engage in, what capabilities future adversaries will bring, and exactly how these conflicts will unfold in the larger global environment. While uncertainty is an intrinsic feature of any sort of planning for the future, it can be difficult to incorporate uncertainty or alternative futures explicitly into defense planning.

No matter which defense planning approach or approaches are used, an ability to assess performance under a variety of different futures and understand the possible range of outcomes is becoming more and more important for strategic planners. The assessment component of any defense planning approach must explore the impact of false assumptions; imperfect information about enemy force structure, capabilities, and plans; and unforeseen changes in the global security environment. Risk may be incorporated in the defense planning process either implicitly or explicitly, or as one of the focuses of the defense planning process itself.

When risks are implicitly managed, decisionmakers make educated assumptions about the variety of possible future states of the world and use these assumptions to make decisions about desired future capabilities, missions, or objectives. When risks are addressed more explicitly, underlying assumptions are tested and sensitivity analyses are conducted. Decisionmakers strive to be aware of the assumptions they are making and attempt to develop an understanding of the impact on operational outcomes if their assumptions are wrong. Many DoD processes are not very good at identifying their assumptions or subjecting them to rigorous analysis. Such analytical methods as simulation or projection of trends into the future can be modified to incorporate changes in base assumptions, yielding information about the sensitivity of future force structure decisions to these assumptions.

The issue of uncertainty is fundamental to defense planning, but it is rarely captured explicitly in the process. The United States must plan forces for an environment whose ultimate threats, opportunities, and demands remain uncertain. The planning process will identify certain assumptions and forecasts, but there is a significant chance these will be wrong—that the nation will end up calling on its military to accomplish missions that it has either downplayed or not identified at all. If a defense planning process assumes that its forecasts and planning factors will be accurate, it will miss these potential effects of uncertainty.

Determining how to incorporate uncertainty into defense planning is a very difficult challenge in practice.[10] It is not immediately obvious what technique would make a defense posture more resilient against multiple possibilities.

One way in which defense planners have tried to incorporate uncertainty into defense planning frameworks is through the use of alternative futures. The use of hedging or alternative futures approaches discourages the use of a single set of threats, objectives, missions, or scenarios as the baseline for the defense plan. Instead, risk- and uncertainty-conscious defense planning incorporates multiple possible scenarios and builds a force that is as successful as possible across the most-significant or -consequential cases. Alternative futures may vary only slightly or quite significantly. For example, on the one hand, alternative views of the world could be based on varying levels of preparedness on the part of our adversaries or degrees of success in implementing a new technology, thus potentially having only small impacts on the required force structure. On the other hand, alternative futures examined could include a completely divergent set of future adversaries exhibiting a widely varying set of threats and capabilities.

Incorporating hedging or alternative futures has both advantages and disadvantages.

Advantages of Incorporating Hedging/Alternative Futures

- It explicitly incorporates risk management into a planning approach, thus encouraging the questioning of assumptions.
- It can (through hedging) identify (and adjust for) situations where incorrect assumptions could lead to catastrophic outcomes.
- It can (through hedging and incorporation of risk) help produce a force that will function well in a variety of future scenarios.

Disadvantages of Hedging/Alternative Futures Approaches

- They can inflate requirements in considering multiple futures, because a future force must perform well in a variety of scenarios.

---

[10] For more details on the difficulty of addressing uncertainty in defense planning, see Michael Fitzsimmons, "The Problem of Uncertainty in Strategic Planning," *Survival*, Vol. 48, No. 4, pp. 131–146, November 2006.

- They can lead to too much investment in capabilities that respond to niche or implausible threats if too much emphasis is placed on risk, thus leading to solutions that are not cost-effective.
- They make prioritization difficult under hedging approaches, because different capabilities or threats may be important across the different future worlds selected.
- They can be costly and difficult to conduct under uncertainty. Whether assessing a future force against a wide variety of scenarios or future worlds or only exploring variations of a single scenario, modeling tools must exist at the correct level of detail. They must be specific enough to provide valuable insights but high-level enough to support multiple analyses within the constrained timeline of a planning cycle.

Summary

In practice, then, any defense planning approach should take elements from both a demand-based and a resource-focused approach and include a discussion of both threats and capabilities.[11] While initial development of strategy requires a focus on desired outcomes, implementation must be grounded in realism about feasibility and affordability. An implementation plan, once devised, must again be assessed against its ability to achieve the desired outcomes. The gap between results of demand-based and resource-focused planning approaches captures how much planners knowingly accept risk. The challenge in successful defense planning lies in assessing capabilities, capacity, and risk using a blended planning approach. No matter what the starting point for planning, the methods that assess a proposed future force's performance in a variety of future scenarios are what ultimately provide valuable information to decisionmakers.

---

[11] See, for example, Troxell, 1997, pp. 12–14, 40. Troxell (1997) notes, "In the end, it is the combination of threat and capability-based planning . . . that will allow the United States to achieve its strategic objectives as currently stated."

CHAPTER THREE

Challenges in Defense Planning Methodology: The Use of Scenarios

Introduction

As discussed in the previous chapter, selecting a high-level defense planning methodology can, to some extent, dictate specific areas of emphasis in defense planning. However, practical defense planning is a mix of several approaches, and its success is heavily contingent on the assessment approaches used in implementation. Defense planning scenarios can play a central role in any of these high-level approaches. Scenarios provide more or less real-world challenges against which a force must be designed: "Any force structure must ultimately be judged against some expected set of operational requirements—those things that the force is expected to be able to do."[1] Scenarios are illustrative potential contingencies that can be used to help inform choices about the size and composition of a joint force. Scenarios can be very specific and determinative—held out as "the" contingencies for which a military is being planned—or they can be more generic and illustrative of the sort of conflicts a military might engage in, even to the point of being built around mythical adversaries. More specifically, scenarios in the U.S. defense planning process are used in at least two somewhat distinct (but potentially complementary) ways: more abstractly and generally to help determine broad Joint Force requirements and in highly detailed and technical terms to conduct operational planning, develop new capability requirements, and test operational concepts.

This chapter surveys challenges with the current approach to the use of scenarios in defense planning.[2] In particular, we are concerned with several questions:

---

[1] Troxell, 1997, p. 14.

[2] There are many complex modeling techniques used to translate specific scenarios into detailed requirements. This report does not discuss that part of the planning process. Its focus is on the strategic-level planning concepts that provide the overall framework for assessing force size and capability requirements.

- What initial process generates the comprehensive list of scenario options?
- How does DoD narrow the range of the universe of potential scenarios to the handful that will be used for force planning? Specifically, what criteria are used to prioritize the scenarios, and how rigorously defined and applied are those criteria?
- How does the process generate the assumptions that help to shape these scenarios and their implications?
- How are the operational concepts chosen that define the character of U.S. missions and requirements relative to the scenarios? Are the choices driven by instrumental considerations,[3] or are broader political and strategic concerns integrated in these phases?
- What purposes do scenarios serve relative to different parts of the planning process?

To answer these questions, we used a qualitative approach. Part of the essential difficulty is that there are no objective measures that can generate evidence for the superiority of one planning *process* over another. Thus, this analysis relies on three sources of evidence to reach its conclusions. One is the lessons of history, as outlined in the Phase One report from this study. A second is a complementary assessment of current approaches, derived from informal dialogues with U.S. defense and Army planners. A third is a process of dialogues with experts in defense planning, including those with extensive experience as practitioners; these included RAND and outside experts. Together, these three lines of analysis produced a number of consistent themes, which form the foundation of this chapter.

We start by discussing the lessons of history and then assess the components of the current DoD defense planning process.

U.S. Historical Experience with Defense Planning

The Phase One report examined the U.S. historical experience with defense planning since 1945.[4] That experience offers a number of lessons that can inform an evaluation of the current scenario development process. Having a sense of how scenarios have been developed and used over time, and of the advantages and risks of various approaches, can help in critiquing how scenarios are developed and used today.

For example, the history of scenario-based planning makes clear that analytical gaps and seams have always existed at various points of the requirements-derivation process, gaps that make the final numbers at least somewhat, perhaps significantly,

---

[3]   Such considerations, for example, as scaling the ambition of CONOPS to current resource constraints or creating a demand signal for forces that reflects the institutional preferences of each military service, rather than focusing on identifying the most appropriate concept for securing U.S. interests.

[4]   Larson, forthcoming.

guesswork. From the international environment to canonical scenarios, in the design of the scenarios, in the identification of assumptions driving their shape, and in the calculation of forces needed to service them, uncertainty creeps in during the process.

In terms of the most general criteria for translating scenarios into requirements, force-sizing constructs have tended to ebb and flow and to embody significant ambiguity. While many defense strategists assert that the ability to simultaneously and decisively win two wars is essential to ensuring that DoD has sufficient forces to deter opportunistic aggression in a second theater when the United States is engaged in a conflict, political leaders seem to have been less concerned with the necessity of a multiple-war criterion. They have repeatedly modified the two-war threshold, with various sizing constructs that set lesser objectives or change the nature of the conflict in the second theater.[5] It is difficult to ascertain whether these changes reflect a desire to explicitly reduce the force-sizing requirements; changes in perspectives on the potential threat and adversary CONOPS; or how the nature and circumstances of a commitment to a first warfight would impact the political decision for the nature of a response in the second theater.

More than that, the political and economic inputs into the process are often as important as the strategic analysis. A common assumption is that the plans and programs of the defense planning process should be strategy-driven, but the final size and shape of the force are highly budget-influenced. The formulation of strategy (and its subgenre, defense planning) necessarily entails a reconciliation of ends, ways, and means in a process of mutual adjustment. Arguably, the United States has never had a force truly capable of meeting the simultaneity-shaped requirements of the full spectrum of scenarios.[6] Even given the best efforts of defense planning professionals, the United States always operates in an ambiguous realm somewhere short of stated requirements.

When operating in that realm, defense planners do not have a reliable way of estimating—or quantifying—risk. The process nominates categories of risk, and services calculate risk against requirements in specific categories, but the criteria for assessing these categories are often highly subjective. The process does not have any objective metrics of risk that could be directly compared and rolled up to allow senior leaders to know just how much risk a given force would represent or how much they would "buy back" with a given increase in resources. This does not mean that DoD is groping entirely in the dark when making significant choices about force structure, readiness, and capability modernization. Rather, it means that translating the "objective" metrics about force and capability sufficiency into a comprehensive assessment of DoD's ability to deliver political objectives in the event of a conflict (as well as the probability

---

5   Conversations with former DoD officials.

6   See, for example, Mackenzie Eaglen and James Talent, "A Clear and Present Danger: QDR Must Recognize Need for Two-War Construct," Heritage Foundation, October 8, 2009.

of the conflict) is resource-intensive and uncertain and involves an irreducible level of judgment.

The historical experience with defense planning also suggests that the major assumptions made in the process play a critical and often unacknowledged or misunderstood role in driving force requirements. Such assumptions as warning time (both in terms of the amount of ambiguous and unambiguous warning, as well as the timeliness of political decisions to respond based on those warnings), simultaneity, mobility, and adversary CONOPS can make massive differences in the requirements generated from the process.

History suggests that the more singular, linear, and predictable the threat profile, the more useful and reliable scenarios can be in generating at least a starting-point set of requirements. However, in an environment of multiple overlapping ambiguous threats and demands, the process of building scenarios may only camouflage inherent uncertainty. In a complex environment, a greater range and complexity of scenarios or subscenario models would seem necessary. Yet, despite the value and detail of some modeling processes used to generate requirements, the defense planning process does not have an established framework or theory for rationalizing its various inputs—the ways that foresight, data, judgment, assumptions, and modeling come together to generate a reliable answer.

In sum, the history of U.S. force planning efforts points to the complex, often subjective nature of the process. There is no example of a purely and reliably objective mechanism for developing and generating requirements for scenarios. In some ways, then, the fact that the current approach does not reflect these characteristics should not come as a surprise. There are however adequate grounds for making reasonable judgments, even in the midst of fundamental uncertainties. The task of the defense planning community is to provide senior decisionmakers with adequate grounds for making those judgments, and there are opportunities to firm up that ground.

Current DoD Defense Planning Processes

At present, defense planning occurs at the service, combatant command (COCOM), joint, and OSD levels. Each component undertakes activities that contribute to the overall process. DoD leadership articulates a defense strategy, key mission areas, and a broad force-sizing and planning framework and, ultimately, decides on the scenarios and integrated combinations of them against which forces will be evaluated. It is not unusual, particularly during times of significant change, for the President to personally set these policies for DoD implementation. Formally, the process—which is called support for strategic analysis (SSA)—is led jointly by the Under Secretary of Defense for Policy, the CJCS, and the director of Cost Assessment and Program Evaluation (CAPE).

Services play an important role in shaping force planning scenarios. Services also adapt the scenarios—which are high level and address only select key force elements—and use them to develop the service force necessary to support the Joint Force elements that are "justified" by the scenarios. Services also use other types of scenarios for concept, doctrine, and material development processes.

Importantly, the scenarios developed in the SSA process are only one of a number of "scenario-like" endeavors that contribute to force development and, ultimately, defense planning. COCOM operational plans (OPLANs), for example—the war plans developed by the warfighting commands—themselves constitute versions of scenarios. They contribute to the development of requirements and the sizing and structuring of forces by providing an additional benchmark for planning. An SSA-developed scenario for a given conflict might suggest certain requirements, for example, but when the COCOM develops its full OPLAN, a new dialogue begins about the needed forces to prevail in the conflict. OPLANs also reflect specific CONOPS for fighting and winning wars, which may produce different requirements from the concepts assumed in a more-generic scenario. OPLANs largely reflect a resource-driven approach, because the combatant commander's staff takes into account current force structure and understanding of the threat to develop the plan. Combatant commanders can highlight risks to the plan, which may either lead to addressing urgent operational needs or feed into the requirements generation process as well, but fundamentally the OPLAN reflects how the Joint Force will address a given threat today, not five years in the future.[7]

Therefore, DoD employs various analytic and procedural methods to derive and constrain the Joint Force size and composition. The overarching framework for synthesizing the sources of risk that the Joint Force will be designed to reduce is called the *force-sizing construct*, while the specific scenarios used to compose a force-sizing construct are called *defense planning scenarios*. The force-sizing construct and associated analysis are characterized by

- the number and combination of contingencies and level of global engagement that the Joint Force should be able to support simultaneously (e.g., two major-theater wars), both in peace and war
- combinations of scenarios representing particular regional or functional challenges to U.S. defense capabilities
- the use of different time horizons—e.g., near, mid, and far—to capture a range of scenarios and different planning mindsets required and to test new concepts and doctrines[8]

---

[7]   Conversations with former DoD operational planners.

[8]   Sometimes, current war plans are used; more typically, scenarios are structured around estimates of what the threat will look like several years into the future, because developing appropriate capabilities or forces frequently takes several years.

- the supporting analysis to focus on either force sufficiency or proficiency, including quantity of units and quality of capability, respectively.

Separately, the building of war plans (i.e., OPLANs and concept plans [CONPLANs]) is led by the COCOMs, with support from the Joint Staff, services, other COCOMs, and oversight from the Office of the Under Secretary of Defense for Policy (OUSD[Policy]).[9]

The development of war plans and defense planning scenarios are related but ultimately distinct elements of the defense planning process. Defense planning scenarios are largely used to examine the adequacy of the programmed Future Years Defense Program (FYDP) force for addressing potential future contingencies that might plausibly occur beyond the FYDP or farther into the future (20 years is a standard time horizon) to encompass future technologies. Defense planning scenarios also help inform research and development priorities, while OPLANs and CONPLANs are used to determine how DoD would respond to a contingency, given current force structure, readiness, and capability constraints. War plans are intended to be resource-constrained (based on service projections of ready forces), while defense planning scenarios are intended to be resource-informed. While OPLAN development is dominated by COCOMs, the services play a more dominant role in the development of the defense planning scenarios (DPSs).

The process to develop scenarios can be long and is influenced by a variety of factors, including the relative novelty of the scenario (i.e., whether it is a completely new scenario or simply a variation of an existing scenario), the number of stakeholders engaged in its development, and level of senior leadership interest. At a high level, the process starts with OUSD(Policy) developing a scenario through a set of engagements with the SSA community that may include one or more tabletop exercises, followed by formal coordination and review of a scenario document. OUSD(Policy) then attempts various forms of developing strategic approaches to address the challenge illustrated in the scenario. This phase can take several months (sometimes up to a year) to complete, depending on the scenario's complexity and level of agreement among the participants on the value of the scenario. Because the scenario is approved at senior levels of DoD (minimally by the SSA tri-chairs, but, at times, scenarios have been approved at the Deputy Secretary level), coordination occurs at multiple levels and over several months. The Joint Staff then leads efforts to develop CONOPS and force requirements to address the scenario's operational challenge. Likewise, this phase can take several months, including convening large, multiday planning conferences with representa-

---

[9]   Gregory Fontenot, E. J. Degen, and David Tohn, *On Point: The United States Army in Operation Iraqi Freedom*, Fort Leavenworth, Kan.: Combat Studies Institute, 2004; Walter J. Perry, Richard E. Darilek, Laurinda L. Rohn, and Jerry M. Sollinger, *Operation IRAQI Freedom: Decisive War, Elusive Peace*, Santa Monica, Calif.: RAND Corporation, RR-1214-A, 2015. OUSD(Policy)'s role in crafting guidance and assisting in plans review is a statutory role in 10 U.S.C. §134.

tives from the services, relevant COCOMs, defense agencies, the Joint Staff, and OSD. Occasionally, these gatherings have also included interagency partners. The Joint Staff then produces a large document (the Multi-Service Force Deployment) that describes the CONOPS by phase and force requirements by functional component command. Finally, a service (or services) can begin detailed analysis based on this document, including use of models and simulation to gain insights on how the warfight might play out, often at the tactical engagement level and showing a day-by-day account of the warfight. These studies can take a year or longer to complete because they require significant computing and human analytic time. It is not unusual, therefore, for a full cycle to take 18 months to 24 months to produce an approved scenario, associated CONOPS, and the start of a detailed campaign analysis.[10]

In recent years, the Joint Staff has instituted a new process called the Joint Military Net Assessment, the purpose of which is to synthesize and integrate the outputs from a variety of planning and analytic processes to inform the CJCS on areas requiring greater attention.[11] This net assessment uses current plans and scenarios, as well as other Joint Strategic Planning System processes, to provide insight into how well the Joint Force is postured to address current and anticipated threats. The net assessment takes existing products as inputs to provide the integrated view, rather than establishing a new process for gathering and analyzing data. This process, unlike the SSA, does not include OSD representation; rather, it feeds into the CJCS's role to provide independent military advice to the Secretary of Defense and the President.

The result of these efforts is a complex, sometimes fragmented process to link national strategic aims and expectations about possible near- and far-term future environments to determinations about needed forces.

Analytical Challenges with the Current Process

Based on the earlier discussion, we offer both high-level findings and some more-specific findings.

High-Level Findings
Our analysis of the current planning process highlights two high-level findings. The first is that the defense planning process is conceptually sound and normally capable of meeting the demands placed on it by senior leaders. DoD, working with the services, has the opportunity to generate a range of scenarios that provide an extensive test for U.S. defense posture. Specific phases in the development process allow for proposals of new scenarios, as well as for alternative courses of action to deal with established ones.

---

[10] Conversations with current and former DoD officials.

[11] Conversations with current DoD officials.

The second finding, however, offers a significant qualification to this general endorsement of the current process: In implementation, the current system is insufficiently timely, flexible, adaptive, and robust. The use of scenarios can, in theory, provide a solid foundation for force planning, serving as guidance about the size and type of forces that will prepare the nation for a range of possible contingencies. In practice, however, serious gaps continue to bedevil the process. First, defense planning currently entails long chains of analysis that depend on judgments and assumptions whose causal links are at times underdefined, unjustified, and—even when specified in strategic guidance for additional analysis—unexamined. Second, the many stages and actors involved in the process, as well as the exhaustive nature of full-scale modeling in support of a force planning scenario, makes it difficult to respond agilely to emerging trends or to test ranges of alternative assumptions or CONOPS. Particularly at the level of analysis involving computer models or the planner-level conferences, the capacity to flexibly dial up or down variables is limited. Moreover, the many layers of bureaucracy tend to quash innovative ideas (either for potential scenarios or for possible adversary or U.S. CONOPS involved in them) and generate both possible contingencies and plans to deal with them that tend to remain in traditional lanes. Third, the final approved canonical scenarios constitute fragile point estimates of possible futures.

The most important question about the scenario process is whether it is giving decisionmakers what they want and need to make high-level judgments. Too narrow a set will not do that. The scenario process should tell compelling stories about a wide range of plausible contingencies and assumptions so that defense planners can work to develop a force that, while not perfect for any one possible war, is not badly mismatched to any potential war. Offering such perspectives to senior decisionmakers can provide them with greater confidence that they are making choices in the presence of the best available information and under conditions of uncertainty. Scenarios, then, are designed to inform senior leadership judgment with the best and most comprehensive perspective on potential contingencies and U.S. responses.

The managers of a scenario development process must also take into account what senior officials *think* they are getting out of the process. Do they, for example, understand the limits of the information they are getting? Do they assume that the answers are objective and reliable? What role do they see for their own judgment in the effort? How much will they rely on the outputs of this process to inform their decisions compared with other sources? When defense planning efforts generate risk assessments specific to precise percentage estimates, they can create false impressions about the reliability of the estimates. But the products of such efforts are not typically explicit about the areas of uncertainty or the margin of error—or the implications of changes in the requirements. The gap between what decisionmakers believe they are getting and what the process can objectively provide can potentially lead to dangerous misunderstandings. Or it can lead decisionmakers to dismiss what they might see as "black box" analysis, one in which the causal dynamics and analytical assumptions are hidden from view.

Our findings suggest that the employment of scenarios in support of defense planning is not in need of a radical overhaul, but important improvements need to be made to enhance its credibility, agility, and robustness. It is challenging to define the criteria that would allow the U.S. defense establishment to be confident of having covered an appropriately wide range of contingencies and from a sufficient number of angles. It is easy to become focused on the details of the process, but the ultimate metric for success is whether the system is producing compelling stories that convey the full range of current and potential threats and gaps in U.S. capabilities to deal with them, and whether the scenarios provide useful and timely analysis to inform the defense planning process.

Specific Findings

The following points outline more-specific findings from our research.

1. The Defense Planning Process Uses Scenarios for a Range of Purposes, Complicating Selection Criteria

In judging whether scenarios have been used effectively, defense leaders must first understand what they are being used to do. Scenarios can be used to support various kinds of decisions, and the degree to which they are effective is relative to their purpose.

Scenarios need to be selected for a wide range of reasons—for example, evaluating Joint Force balance; examining various factors, such as readiness and modernization; and more.

Strategic guidance uses scenarios to create a list of generic capabilities. Threat analyses use scenarios to assess capacity. Any given set of capabilities—for weapons of mass destruction mitigation, area security, or combined-arms combat—that is required in one scenario may be vastly different in scale and composition than a set used in another scenario. But if only one scenario will be run through the entirety of the planning process, this one scenario will be used to determine force size overall. Questions of force mix *across* scenarios may be difficult to include in the rest of the process. When a service shows that it needs a more-robust depth of capability in a different environment to do a specific mission than is allowed in the "low risk" (or "medium risk") solution for the chosen mix of scenarios, there is no effective way to discuss the structure trades.

2. The Primary Challenges in Using Scenarios Reside in Their Practical Implementation, not in the Overall Structure of the Process

Systems, such as the Joint Planning System and the Planning, Programming, Budgeting, and Execution System (PPBES), provide all the necessary steps in developing requirements for conventional forces. There is nothing fundamentally wrong with the systems' design or approach. For example, the processes themselves allow for including all the scenarios that senior leaders feel are necessary. These planning processes are not inherently restrictive by their design, and analysts are encouraged, by the nature of the process, to experiment with various parameters to determine the sensitivity of results to specific capabilities or capacities. Most of the challenges arise in the way the process is actually conducted.

The process has two phases—selecting scenarios that will test a proposed force and assessing those scenarios through modeling and other means—and challenges occur in executing the two phases. In its review of defense planning processes, the U.S. Government Accountability Office (GAO) has emphasized that high-level assumptions are critical in determining the outcomes of scenario-based planning exercises.[12] The current process already pays significant attention to the choice of assumptions, but it lacks time and resources to adequately explore the implications of these assumptions. As the GAO emphasizes, these assumptions can often drive outcomes. Scenario-building and assessment must include detailed consideration of assumptions, including sensitivity analysis.

In selecting scenarios to underpin planning purposes, assumptions may limit the scenarios considered and make it difficult to cover an appropriately wide range of possible futures. Any specific number of conflicts can become an arbitrary planning function. There are any number of potential wars the United States could fight, and the compound probability of some of them occurring simultaneously is rarely seriously examined. Therefore, choosing to size or prepare for two or two-plus-one or any other number of scenarios involves guesswork rather than meaningful strategic judgment. In addition, a scenario can play a vital role in understanding the attributes the force might need at the same time that senior leadership determines it is not appropriate for force-sizing. For example, a large-scale stabilization operation in the interior of a continent would test the ability to project and sustain forces in an austere environment while conducting complex, but not high-end combat, operations. DoD leadership may determine that this scenario is sufficiently different from the other scenarios to be useful for capabilities development or strategy analysis, while simultaneously determining that it is inappropriate for sizing the Army or other services.

Some potentially flawed assumptions can continue to be made across all or most of the scenarios, even in the face of significant changes in the security environment. Planners may also be reluctant to discard outdated scenarios. Too much focus on risk and hedging, and the inclusion of too many potentially outdated or irrelevant scenarios, can then lead to very high cost to cover worst-case outcomes.

---

[12] GAO, *Quadrennial Defense Review: 2010 Report Addressed Many but Not All Required Items*, Washington, D.C., GAO-10-575R, April 30, 2010.

3. The Quality and Utility of the Process Are Functions of Senior Leadership Engagement and Commitment

The existing structure and process of the scenario-testing function can work very well and have worked well at various times. The function can both inform senior leaders about the sufficiency of planned forces against proposed contingencies and test alternative missions and CONOPS. But recent history suggests that it will only work well, or even adequately, when it enjoys strong support and engagement from senior leaders.

This engagement can come in many forms. Senior leaders can make clear their general support for the process. They can become personally involved in designing and selecting scenarios. They can aid the process of checking for assumptions and forcing consideration of multiple excursions. They can devote significant time and resources to the activity as symbols of their commitment. Most of all, senior leaders can make choices—and publicly indicate that they have made these choices—informed by DoD's assessments of the planning outcomes.

4. The Process of Narrowing to a Handful of Force Planning Scenarios Can Be Subjective and Arbitrary

The process of scenario development should begin by identifying a wide range of potential scenarios—dozens or more. This is meant to be the full range of contingencies that might plausibly arise in the strategic environment. Immediately, however, the goal is to narrow down to a small number of illustrative scenarios or scenario combinations. The planning process is not built to develop or assess a large number of scenarios; the force planning and analytic communities do not have the time or resources to do so; and the way scenarios are used today involves large amounts of detail that make every scenario analysis extremely time-consuming and resource-intensive.

Given this, an early step in the process involves narrowing down the choices to a representative few and then taking those scenarios and decreasing the potential combinations into a handful that then provide the basis for defense planning.

But this narrowing process does not operate according to any clear or objective criteria, at least not in practice.[13] This is true at both major stages—the narrowing of scenarios and the combining of scenarios into ISCs. OSD provides detailed guidance for developing specific scenarios, but the process of decreasing from many to a few and then assembling those few scenarios into ISCs is necessarily subjective. The "down-selecting" to a smaller number of scenarios takes place under the guidance of senior leadership judgment, based on the perceived plausibility of scenarios and the extent to which they are seen as representative of the class of challenges that U.S. forces are expected to encounter in the future. These judgments can sometimes ratify conventional wisdom and preclude a wider range of scenarios viewed as less likely and/or less representative. Senior defense leaders are inevitably—and understandably—preoccupied with the

---

[13] Conversations with former DoD officials familiar with the process.

challenges immediately in front of them and generally less interested in thinking about long-range or out-of-the-box scenarios.

Our analysis agrees with many studies that have pointed to the importance of increasing the "scenario space" within the overall process and of not allowing choices during implementation to unnecessarily constrain the contingencies being examined.[14] However, the problem is not simply that the current number of scenarios is too small. They may be sufficient in number and range, depending on what criteria are used to determine the sufficiency of scenarios. The bigger problem is that the framework of assessment, sufficiency, modeling, and force planning tools are not set up to handle excursions around the base scenarios.[15] While it may make sense to focus on a few critical scenarios involving specific potential adversaries, it becomes much more difficult to address how each of these conflicts might unfold, exactly what is needed to conduct the campaigns under various potential alternative futures, and how they relate to one another in terms of generating demand. Senior leaders' desire to examine the effects of key assumptions and alternative strategies indicate that what is needed are not necessarily more scenarios but more versions of the scenario cases.

This occurs to some degree now, with wargaming and shorter excursions that do not demand full-scale modeling and requirements development. However, it remains incomplete and haphazard in application. The process does not have a formalized middle tier of analysis between very rough scenario descriptions and full-scale modeling.

A related problem is that the actual implementation of the planning processes tends to emphasize the conflicts familiar to U.S. planners and defense leaders rather than to anticipate the unfamiliar. This includes both types of conflict and specific contingencies. Combined with the tendency of military institutions under budgetary pressures to address pressing near-term needs, the result is to prioritize the present over the future in often unbalanced ways.

Thus, the potential for very different future contingencies or breakthrough technologies can be systematically underemphasized. DoD could benefit from placing greater emphasis on nonstandard scenarios rather than focusing energy on long-term deliberate planning for one or two expected ones. Until the recent Russian invasion of Crimea, many experts believed that a future ground war between major military powers was deeply implausible for the foreseeable future. Much of the focus was on preparing for conflict in predominantly maritime and air environments, such as the Western Pacific. This led DoD to shift away, both in terms of analytic focus and actual budgetary investments, from ground forces and to increasingly focus on air and sea

---

[14]   Paul K. Davis, *Capabilities for Joint Analysis in the Department of Defense: Rethinking Support for Strategic Analysis*, Santa Monica, Calif.: RAND Corporation, 2016, pp. 37–38; Charles Roxburgh, "The Use and Abuse of Scenarios," McKinsey and Company, November 2009.

[15]   Davis, 2016.

battles, based on an assumption that ground wars involving large-scale mechanized forces were becoming less common and less plausible.

Standard scenarios are offered as examples, but, as Davis and Finch noted, by making them so central to planning,

> planners will come to treat them as predictive, as though they believe them, and will develop mental attitudes, analytical constructs, and procedures making rapid adaptation in large-scale crisis difficult. Empirically, we know that calling the scenarios "illustrative" has never solved this problem, because organizations yearn for concreteness and the "test cases" become "the" cases.[16]

Therefore, the use of "stressing scenarios" is misleading, because some scenarios stress different capabilities than others. The Joint Force might pass one stress test and fail another.

5. The Assessment of Scenarios Has Become So Exhaustive and Inflexible That It Constrains the Responsiveness of the Overall Process

Our analysis suggests that a significant problem is the depth and sophistication with which scenarios are typically examined. Ultimately, to furnish guidance for requirements and force design, a small number of scenarios is examined at exhaustive levels of detail. Because the outcomes need to feed a variety of highly data-centric models, scenarios tend to be highly developed, enormously complex, and highly specified. The time commitment required to generate or modify any particular scenario introduces significant inflexibility into the system. The focus tends toward getting the scenarios "right," rather than conducting analysis on a set of plausible scenarios.

There could be other options, as we suggest next, but this is the practice today, in part because of a built-in catch-22 in the process: Senior leaders want to consider a wide range of issues, but they will not approve scenarios for deeper analysis until they are thoroughly vetted, which itself demands considerable time and effort. The result is to lock the process into a small group of scenarios that reflect conventional wisdom about future warfighting challenges. The combined effect is that all significant force structure debates center around a single specific future and a single set of desired outcomes, such as appears to have occurred in the 2014 QDR.

Our analysis suggests that this slow responsiveness and lack of flexibility are among the greatest impediments to a more-effective and responsive defense planning process. While scenario-based approaches can help to define threats and goals specifically, aid in prioritization, and provide a tangible focus for defense planning, the labor and time required for scenario development means that only a small set of scenarios are created as part of a given planning effort. Once established, it becomes difficult to challenge or question underlying scenario assumptions. The belief that scenario creation

---

[16] Davis and Finch, 1993.

necessarily reduces risk of surprise is flawed. Risk is still inherent in the assumptions underlying the scenario, but such risk becomes more difficult to see once a scenario is agreed on by all stakeholders.

As a result, when using scenarios or contingencies, the process tends to rely on ones that are years old and have difficulty responding to rapidly changing characteristics in the strategic environment. The slow response to growing Russian challenges in Eastern Europe is a good recent example. Such sluggishness is especially problematic because it makes it much more difficult for the planning process to justify investments over the long term, including slow-developing "game-changing" technologies or capabilities.

The high cost and complexity of scenarios also tend to mean that individual planning exercises have massive import; thus, services know that they only get "one shot" and will fight hard to ensure that the scenario sheds the best light (and highest demand) on their ability to contribute. Adjudicating all of that effort also eats up staff and, increasingly, leadership time. This has the pernicious effect of unduly lengthening the scenario development process (thus exacerbating the bandwidth problem) because almost without fail senior leadership injects new assumptions or constraints into the scenarios well after the SSA process is under way; this requires the defense planning process to hit "rewind," often multiple times. It also results in spending more time on establishing the "starting point" for analysis, rather than conducting the analysis itself.[17]

An alternative approach might include a more-fundamental review of what analytic questions the scenarios are intended to address and whether DoD is burdening the scenarios with expectations to "be all things to all people." Clearly, the scenarios, their CONOPS, and force lists play an important role in addressing broad force-sizing and shaping questions, but, as noted earlier, the resulting analysis is highly dependent on the assumptions. For example, the degree of overlap between fights in the two major theater war construct is a significant driver of the demands on the Joint Force. Simultaneous wars with short warning times are highly stressing because of the need for rapid deployment (or forward deployment) of significant forces and the stacking of demands at the height of the third phase of operations. On the other hand, if the wars are sufficiently separated in terms of peak demand, then the ability to swing forces alleviates some of the stress. The demands in the fourth phase (stabilization) and associated assumptions, such as whether allies and partners will carry some of the demand, are additional critical factors.

Developing and testing alternative concepts, on the other hand, might be better addressed through wargaming that can more easily vary base assumptions. This competition of concepts could be used to screen alternatives before more-detailed analysis is conducted using SSA. Wargames and simple models can also usefully and rela-

---

[17] Conversations with DoD officials.

tively quickly test the sensitivity of assumptions, such as basing access or warning time. Finally, for capabilities development, it may be sufficient to evaluate the desired attributes of a new system or platform using more-general descriptions of operating environments (e.g., high desert versus Arctic circle), rather than have a detailed scenario description that describes the conflict or vignette.[18] SSA would still play a role in addressing how much of a new capability to acquire.

6. The Organizational Support Structure for the Scenario Analysis Processes Has Been Significantly Degraded

In recent years, DoD has dismantled the joint community's only capability for conducting campaign modeling analysis, which had resided in OSD CAPE. The decision was catalyzed by manning reductions in CAPE, which reduced the number of scenarios and variations of each scenarios DoD can consider. More broadly, DoD leadership made the decision to disband CAPE's campaign modeling capabilities because senior leaders felt the results were not credible, because of the opacity of assumptions driving outcomes, and—perhaps, more troubling—because of their failure to pass simple sensitivity analysis tests. In the two most-recent force planning efforts (2012 and 2014), DoD relied on OPLANs as the bases for assessing capacity demands and on extrapolations of previous scenario assessments, as well as service-generated campaign analyses, to evaluate the capabilities of programmed forces.[19]

This problem magnifies the other problems noted earlier. It means that the challenge posed by exhaustive scenario analysis becomes even more debilitating, and the capacity to test various operational concepts becomes even more limited.

These organizational shortcomings have a number of specific implications. They reduce the quality of sensitivity analysis, because the capabilities simply do not exist to conduct multiple different iterations. The scenario-building process has formally changed the level of analysis conducted to evaluate specific contingencies as a result of the declining capabilities, and this cannot fail to affect the perceived availability of bandwidth to assess different versions of scenarios and U.S. responses. These shortcomings do not necessarily argue for rejuvenating the full-scale, exhaustive campaign models that had been in place before: The skepticism of senior leaders about their results was, in part, justified. But it does point again to the need for an intermediate-phase or depth-of-scenario analysis—something between back-of-the-envelope guesswork and exhaustive (sometimes yearslong) modeling.

The decline in resources for large-scale campaign modeling has perhaps had one unintended benefit. Without the ability to conduct massive, detailed modeling exercises, force planners have increasingly had to turn to more-streamlined wargaming and

---

[18] These changes would likely require agreement across OSD, the Joint Staff, and the services and reviews of DoD Directives, Instructions, and other guidance that may direct the use of the SSA process or its outputs.

[19] Conversations with former DoD officials.

simulations to test proposed forces. This, in turn, has offered the ability for the process to become more responsive, albeit less rigorous. The use of quick-turn wargames appears to have become more common since 2014, for example, especially when applied to emerging contingencies.

7. Operational Concepts Arbitrarily Overdetermine Requirements Derived from a Given Scenario or Force-Sizing Construct

A related challenge in defense planning comes from the role of operational concepts in shaping the purported requirements of different scenarios. Once threats and scenarios have been identified, planners must make assumptions about how U.S. forces would fight the conflict. Different CONOPS can have vastly distinct implications for the number and type of forces that a given scenario would require. A significant challenge with the current system is that while there are, in theory, opportunities to discuss and test various CONOPS, in practice there is often insufficient time for in-depth development of many of these—and the process tends to weed out innovative concepts as it goes along. One implication is that the requirements produced by scenarios are at least somewhat arbitrary, because they do not reflect a full debate about how to deal with the demand.

In theory, the process could embody several to dozens of alternative "runs," each reflecting a different operating concept. In practice, however, while lower-fidelity wargaming is sometimes used for this purpose (especially in the COCOMs in the development of war plans), the testing of multiple CONOPS is not an institutionalized element of the planning process.

Although a variety of courses of action (COAs) and CONOPS may have been developed and analyzed in scenario development, only one survives, and there is no usable record of the alternate COA/CONOPS that were considered. Those who would propose new ways to fight a given contingency face a dilemma: The system will often refuse to approve in-depth consideration of an operating concept until it is "proven"; but it cannot be proven without that analytical effort. The result is that the planning system tends to lock onto existing CONOPS as much as it does current scenarios. All measurements of risk are then measured against that outcome. Such an approach gives little guidance to an effort to allocate resources among competing demand signals.

8. The Definition of Success in the Scenarios Is Often Left Unexamined

In many examples of defense planning since Operation Desert Storm, the authors of scenarios set ambitious standards and timelines for the achievement of key operational objectives. The resulting requirements then demonstrate what is needed for the force to achieve potentially very extensive outcomes on a very demanding timeline.

What is often lost in the process is a sense of how relatively modest changes in the definition of success would affect requirements. Participants in past efforts have described situations in which altering required timelines by only a few short weeks made tremendous differences in the forces required to achieve the objectives. In fact, comparing forces required to achieve different versions of success ought to be a central preoccupation of senior leaders: What they think they need to achieve in each scenario is a fundamental component of strategic judgment. Therefore, the process ought to examine such distinctions and equip senior leaders to make informed decisions about how much success they need and at what cost and risk.

Summary

In sum, we conclude that the basic structure and approach of the force planning process are effective in achieving its goals in the aggregate. The existing process gives senior leaders an opportunity to test specific proposed force designs against detailed contingencies. It creates an ongoing dialogue about the contingencies most likely to demand U.S. military responses. And increasingly over the past year, more-responsive wargaming techniques have become more common. The process is not broken, in other words, and generates significant insight that can contribute to senior leadership judgment about force design.

However, the process still suffers from two notable flaws that constrain its effectiveness. First, despite recent changes, it is still not responsive enough to quickly adapt to changes in the strategic environment and offer robust but quick-turn findings on the demands of newly arising contingencies. This problem may become even more worrisome as we enter a period of significant global turbulence, when new demand signals could arise at any moment. Second, the process tends to narrow into singular "approved solutions" that arbitrarily constrain the consideration of alternative forms contingencies might take or distinct operating concepts the United States might adopt in dealing with them. The next chapter offers a number of recommendations designed to enhance the current process in these two respects.

CHAPTER FOUR

Conclusions and Recommendations

This chapter draws on previous findings to make a number of recommendations for improving the current defense planning process. We recommend DoD adapt its defense planning capabilities to explore noncanonical scenarios, explore canonical scenarios in fresh and innovative ways, prioritize scenarios for analysis beyond the force-sizing construct, and assess the implications of critical assumptions.

Conclusions

Broadly speaking, the most fundamental conclusion of our analysis is that the process is structurally sound but insufficiently flexible. In theory, many opportunities, methods, and means exist to respond to a changing security environment—including scenario or war plan "in progress reviews" with the Secretary of Defense and his advisers, wargaming, and the development of alternative CONOPS. In practice, however, the layers of approval required for new CONOPS, lengthy intradepartmental coordination, exhaustive detail required for the preferred formal modeling, and the resource-intensiveness of the entire process—even as headquarters shrink—often make the system unable to generate new scenarios and concepts for an area of interest in a timely manner.[1] Instead, DoD ends up with a single new authoritative scenario—a point solution rather than an exploration of the many policy-relevant differences in the way a conflict might unfold.

Just as important, the process both obscures critical uncertainties and smothers innovation in a process that tends to be unwelcoming to innovative or controversial ideas or initiatives that might delay decisions about the new canonical scenario still further. This process can work during times of continuity (scenario diversity is developed over several years), but during times of sudden discontinuity, it seriously erodes DoD's responsiveness.

---

[1] The closing of Joint Forces Command also negatively affected DoD's ability and capacity to experiment with new concepts.

Recommendations

Our recommendations are largely oriented around these challenges and around the eight specific findings presented in Chapter Three.

Explore a Broader Set of Low-Fidelity Scenarios to Hedge Against Surprise

The process could benefit from competitively developing a range of ideas and concepts. To address the fundamental challenge that the process gets stuck on the same set of scenarios, we could use a "scenario skunkworks" that constantly generates scenarios, contingencies, alternative CONOPS, key assumptions, or other distinct ways of defining and approaching problems for in-depth assessment and then offers them as candidates for possible comprehensive treatment. This team could serve as scouts exploring the geostrategic horizon.

This recommendation points to the potential value of two tiers of analysis: one that is more exhaustive and complete, such as the detailed modeling in the current system, for all the purposes of scenarios; and another that is more streamlined, for consideration of newer and more-experimental scenarios and CONOPS applied to them. The more-agile approach would offer a proof-of-concept test bed for potential contingencies and CONOPS. This approach would likely require rules regarding the appropriate use of each scenario for force-sizing, force-shaping, strategy analysis, CONOPS development and experimentation, and capabilities development.

Part of the argument for an ability to assess a wider range of scenarios is that the system relies on senior leadership judgment to distinguish plausible from implausible contingencies. In some cases, those evaluating proposed scenarios will use current defense planning guidelines to make their choices, but those guidelines are again focused on current missions. That judgment is grounded in experience and current ways of seeing the world, which may wrongly exclude future possibilities. The execution of the process needs an opportunity for conceptual entrepreneurs to bring forward contingencies that may seem unlikely at the time but that may prove central to Army and Joint Force missions at a later period. The best way to assess and hedge against a wide range of threats is to consider a wide range of contingencies.

Explore Current Scenarios with a Focus on Innovation

A second front of exploration would be to approach current scenarios with an eye toward innovation. Rather than being drawn into disputes over institutional interests, this second initiative would bring Joint, cross-functional teams to bear on crucial operational dilemmas. While the focus of the team discussed in the previous recommendation would be on identifying underappreciated threats to the national security strategy, this group's focus would be on underappreciated opportunities to achieve desired outcomes in challenging contingencies. The U.S. Naval War College's Halsey Alpha and

Bravo Groups could serve as an initial benchmark for how this kind of capability could be designed and how it should perform.[2]

In pursuing these goals, DoD could consider creating structural mechanisms to ensure a regular supply of innovative thinking on operational concepts. Defense analyst Glenn Kent proposed one such idea, which he termed "conceiver's action groups" or "concept options groups."[3] He described these as teams of roughly 15 people formed to brainstorm innovative conceptual solutions to specific operational problems. They would include both technologists and officers with operational backgrounds to generate a dialogue about solutions that are both technologically feasible and operationally effective. However, part of the motivation was also to produce a new source of creativity within a process that too often can be hamstrung by existing plans and assumptions. Formalizing something like Kent's concept action groups, perhaps at both the OSD-Joint Staff and service levels, would at least create an opportunity for more alternative approaches to be developed and considered.

In that spirit, the exploratory work recommended here and above is often better pursued outside the immediate institutional decision processes and cycles. DoD should seriously consider establishing these two capabilities within such an institution as the National Defense University, leveraging the high-quality students it receives from across the Joint Force. Just as the Halsey Groups brief the Chief of Naval Operations annually, it would be desirable for this defense planning innovation group to brief the Secretary or Deputy Secretary of Defense and CJCS or Vice CJCS annually on its findings, as well as to receive guidance on where future efforts should focus. During the same briefing cycle, it would be desirable for either the National Defense University or one of the SSA principals to sponsor a conference for discussing these and related topics—to create an environment in which difficult issues can be discussed frankly without the typical immediacy of supporting senior leaders' decisions and bureaucratic competition.

Anticipate Disruption; Prioritize Beyond the Force Sizing Construct

The current process is not as responsive as it could be because it is not designed to anticipate scenarios that *could* emerge at some future point. It should not have come as a surprise, for example, that Russia was turning against the West in ways that would generate new potential planning scenarios and possible force requirements. Yet, the

---

[2] For a description of the Halsey Groups, see U.S. Naval War College, "Special Programs," webpage, undated.

[3] For discussions of the concept, see Glenn A. Kent, David Ochmanek, Michael Spirtas, and Bruce R. Pirnie, *Thinking About America's Defense: An Analytical Memoir*, Santa Monica, Calif.: RAND Corporation, OP-223-AF, 2008, p. 245; and John Birkler, C. Richard Neu, and Glenn A. Kent, *Gaining New Military Capability: An Experiment in Concept Development*, Santa Monica, Calif.: RAND Corporation, MR-912-OSD, 1998, pp. xii, 5, 15–16. In Kent's original conception, these groups would address mostly operational issues. He was not envisioning groups that would play a role in scenario generation, but the idea could perhaps be relevant to the focus of this study.

Russian threat to the Baltics emerged suddenly in the wake of the Ukraine conflict, and defense planners scrambled to respond in a timely manner. Senior leaders are well aware that the few scenarios chosen as benchmarks for force planning are only a small subset of the much wider universe of scenarios suggested, defined, and developed at various levels of detail. The problem is not that the current process does not have the room to add new possible contingencies to various lists. It is that it does not consciously and specifically highlight a second smaller number for attention as future risks.

For example, merely for illustrative purposes, suppose that at a given time the broadest list of scenarios included contingencies ranging from humanitarian operations in South Asia to a significant redeployment to Iraq to stability operations in Syria or postcollapse North Korea, as well as two dozen more such cases. [4] The planning process cannot evaluate all of them with equal fidelity, but it could have a function designed to highlight three or four of them, through a combination of intelligence indicators and senior leadership judgment, that OSD and the services agree should join the top-tier list of day-to-day benchmarking scenarios. These could then be discussed and debated in terms of the various forms they could take, the CONOPS that the United States could choose to deal with them, and the potential force requirements. These would not be full-scale scenario analyses; rather they would be initial, rough-cut looks that would streamline the process of more-complete examination if and when senior leaders made that determination.

Assess the Impact of Critical Assumptions and Choices

DoD typically identifies the assumptions involved in many defense decision processes, but they are sometimes offered as a quick, almost throw-away initial phase to the process. Often, the key assumptions do not become the subject of significant discussion, because they reflect taken-for-granted conventional wisdom and beliefs. For example, scenarios will make assumptions about the role of partners and allies in certain contingencies largely based on internal experts' opinions, rather than engaging those partners directly in the process. Moreover, planning processes do not always identify the specific implications of assumptions for the final result—What proportion of the final demand signal is the result of assumptions? Acknowledging assumptions is not enough—against which they must be assessed.

A revised process could take the assumption phase more seriously. It could subject assumptions to rigorous analysis and debate and force the system to take seriously the implications of its conventional wisdom. It also could inform this discussion with a more-detailed estimate of the relationship between specific assumptions and outcomes.

---

[4] These are simply illustrative; we do not mean to suggest that these or any other specific scenarios form part of the current planning set.

As suggested in the previous chapter, a significant shortcoming of the current process is that it gives insufficient attention to two critical sources of uncertainty and variability in planning outcomes: alternative definitions of success, and alternative CONOPS for performing stated missions. Each of these can have dramatic effects on the outcomes of analysis. More important, however, making these judgments—what the United States is trying to accomplish in a potential conflict or mission, and how it will go about achieving that result—ranks among the most important aspects of senior leadership strategic judgment. The defense planning process must inform such judgments with a range of alternatives for each scenario—what different concepts of success and operational concepts would mean for the number and type of forces and capabilities needed. Only by comparing such options in detail can senior leaders make fully informed judgments about force posture.

This will demand the sort of middle-tier analytical capabilities mentioned earlier. The current process would not be able to generate meaningful findings about the implications of multiple operational concepts or concepts of success for multiple scenarios. Conducting such a range of analyses would overload the system.

Our study has identified both strengths and weaknesses of the current process for conceiving, generating, and employing scenarios in support of defense planning decisions. That process offers significant insight to senior decisionmakers and serves many of its core purposes in identifying key requirements for success in specific contingencies. However, this analysis has also discovered a number of modest but important changes to the process, mostly in the area of its flexibility and focus on unusual and surprise scenarios, that could further improve the insights it offers to senior defense decisionmakers attempting to prioritize among limited resources.

Bibliography

Bartlett, Henry, "Approaches to Force Planning," in the Force Planning Faculty, ed., *Fundamentals of Force Planning*: Vol. 1, *Concepts*, Naval War College, 1990.

Birkler, John, C. Richard Neu, and Glenn A. Kent, *Gaining New Military Capability: An Experiment in Concept Development*, Santa Monica, Calif.: RAND Corporation, MR-912-OSD, 1998. As of January 17, 2018:
https://www.rand.org/pubs/monograph_reports/MR912.html

Chairman of the Joint Chiefs of Staff, *Management and Review of Joint Strategic Capabilities Plan (JSCP)-Tasked Plans*, Washington, D.C., CJCS Instruction 3141.01E, current as of September 8, 2014a.

———, *Campaign Planning Procedures and Responsibilities*, Washington, D.C., CJCS Manual 3130.01A, November 25, 2014b.

———, *Contingency Planning Supplement to the 2015 Joint Strategic Capabilities Plan (JSCP)*, Washington, D.C., CJCS Instruction 3110.01J-1, September 25, 2015a, not available to the public.

———, *Joint Strategic Planning System*, Washington, D.C., CJCS Instruction 3100.01C, November 20, 2015b.

Condit, Kenneth W., *The Joint Chiefs of Staff and National Policy*, Vol. VI, *1955–1956*, Washington, D.C.: Joint Chiefs of Staff, Joint History Office, 1992.

———, *The Joint Chiefs of Staff and National Policy*, Vol. II, *1947–1949*, Washington, D.C.: Joint Chiefs of Staff, Joint History Office, 1996.

Davis, Paul K., ed., *New Challenges for Defense Planning: Rethinking How Much Is Enough*, Santa Monica, Calif.: RAND Corporation, MG-400-RC, 1994. As of January 29, 2018:
https://www.rand.org/pubs/monograph_reports/MR400.html

———, *Capabilities for Joint Analysis in the Department of Defense: Rethinking Support for Strategic Analysis*, Santa Monica, Calif.: RAND Corporation, RR-1469-OSD, 2016. As of January 16, 2018:
https://www.rand.org/pubs/research_reports/RR1469.html

Davis, Paul K., and Lou Finch, *Defense Planning for the Post–Cold War Era: Giving Meaning to Flexibility, Adaptiveness, and Robustness of Capability*, Santa Monica, Calif.: RAND Corporation, MR-322-JS, 1993. As of January 29, 2018:
https://www.rand.org/pubs/monograph_reports/MR322.html

DoD—*See* U.S. Department of Defense.

Eaglen, Mackenzie, and James Talent, "A Clear and Present Danger: QDR Must Recognize Need for Two-War Construct," Heritage Foundation, October 8, 2009. As of July 3, 2017:
http://www.heritage.org/budget-and-spending/commentary/
clear-and-present-danger-qdr-must-recognize-need-two-war-construct

Fairchild, Byron R., and Walter S. Poole, *The Joint Chiefs of Staff and National Policy*, Vol. VII, *1957–1960*, Washington, D.C.: Joint Chiefs of Staff, Joint History Office, 2000.

Fitzsimmons, Michael, "The Problem of Uncertainty in Strategic Planning," *Survival*, Vol. 48, No. 4, November 2006, pp. 131–146.

Fontenot, Gregory, E. J. Degen, and David Tohn, *On Point: The United States Army in Operation Iraqi Freedom*, Fort Leavenworth, Kan.: Combat Studies Institute, 2004.

GAO—*See* U.S. Government Accountability Office.

Gunzinger, Mark, *Shaping America's Future Military*, Washington, D.C.: Center for Strategic and Budgetary Assessments, 2013. As of January 25, 2018:
http://csbaonline.org/research/publications/
shaping-americas-future-military-toward-a-new-force-planning-construct

Hadley, Stephen, and William Perry, *The QDR in Perspective: Meeting America's National Security Needs in the 21st Century—Final Report of the Quadrennial Defense Review Independent Panel*, Washington, D.C.: United States Institute of Peace, 2010. As of June 27, 2017:
https://www.usip.org/sites/default/files/qdr/qdrreport.pdf

Hicks, Kathleen H., and Samuel J. Brannen, "Force Planning in the 2010 QDR," *Joint Forces Quarterly*, No. 59, 4th Quarter, 2010.

Joint Chiefs of Staff, "Description of the Joint Strategic Planning System (JSPS)," briefing, Washington, D.C., July 2009. As of January 17, 2018:
http://dde.carlisle.army.mil/LLL/DSC/ppt/L13_JSPS.pdf

Kent, Glenn A., David Ochmanek, Michael Spirtas, and Bruce R. Pirnie, *Thinking About America's Defense: An Analytical Memoir*, Santa Monica, Calif.: RAND Corporation, OP-223-AF, 2008. As of January 17, 2018:
https://www.rand.org/pubs/occasional_papers/OP223.html

Kent, Glenn A., and William E. Simons, "Objective-Based Planning," in Paul K. Davis, ed., *New Challenges for Defense Planning: Rethinking How Much Is Enough*, Santa Monica, Calif.: RAND Corporation, MR-400-RC, 1994. As of January 17, 2018:
https://www.rand.org/pubs/monograph_reports/MR400.html

Kugler, Richard L., "Nonstandard Contingencies for Defense Planning," in Paul K. Davis, ed., *New Challenges for Defense Planning: Rethinking How Much Is Enough*, Santa Monica, Calif.: RAND Corporation, MG-400-RC, 1994. As of January 18, 2018:
https://www.rand.org/pubs/monograph_reports/MR400.html

Larson, Eric V., *Force Planning Scenarios, 1945–2016: Their Origins and Use in Defense Strategic Planning*, Santa Monica, Calif.: RAND Corporation, RR-2173-A, forthcoming.

Larson, Eric V., Derek Eaton, Michael E. Linick, John E. Peters, Agnes Gereben Schaefer, Keith Walters, Stephanie Young, H. G. Massey, and Michelle Darrah Ziegler, *Defense Planning in a Time of Conflict: A Comparative Analysis of the 2001–2014 Quadrennial Defense Reviews, and Implications for the Army*, Santa Monica, Calif.: RAND Corporation, RR-1309-A, 2018. As of February 9, 2018:
https://www.rand.org/pubs/research_reports/RR1309.html

Meinhart, Richard, *Strategic Planning by the Chairmen, Joint Chiefs of Staff, 1990 to 2005*, Carlisle Barracks, Pa.: Strategic Studies Institute, U.S. Army War College, April 2006.

Office of the Under Secretary of Defense (Comptroller), *Fiscal Year 2017 President's Budget: The Joint Staff*, Washington, D.C., February 2016.

Perry, Walter L., Richard E. Darilek, Laurinda L. Rohn, and Jerry M. Sollinger, *Operation IRAQI FREEDOM: Decisive War, Elusive Peace*, Santa Monica, Calif.: RAND Corporation, RR-1214-A, 2015. As of January 17, 2018:
https://www.rand.org/pubs/research_reports/RR1214.html

Poole, Walter S., *The Evolution of the Joint Strategic Planning System, 1947–1989*, Washington, D.C.: Historical Division, Joint Secretariat, Joint Staff, September 1989.

———, *The Joint Chiefs of Staff and National Policy*, Vol. IV, *1950–1952*, Washington, D.C.: Joint Chiefs of Staff, Joint History Office, 1998.

———, *The Joint Chiefs of Staff and National Policy*, Vol. VIII, *1961–1964*, Washington, D.C.: Joint Chiefs of Staff, Joint History Office, 2011.

———, *The Joint Chiefs of Staff and National Policy*, Vol. IX, *1965–1968*, Washington, D.C.: Joint Chiefs of Staff, Joint History Office, 2012.

———, *The Joint Chiefs of Staff and National Policy*, Vol. X, *1969–1972*, Washington, D.C.: Joint Chiefs of Staff, Joint History Office, 2013.

———, *The Joint Chiefs of Staff and National Policy*, Vol. XI, *1973–1976*, Washington, D.C.: Joint Chiefs of Staff, Joint History Office, 2015.

Rearden, Steven L., *Council of War: A History of the Joint Chiefs of Staff, 1942–1991*, Washington, D.C.: Joint Chiefs of Staff, Joint History Office, 2012.

Rearden, Steven L., and Kenneth R. Foulks, *The Joint Chiefs of Staff and National Policy*, Vol. XII, *1977–1980*, Washington, D.C.: Joint Chiefs of Staff, Joint History Office, 2015.

Record, Jeffrey, *The Creeping Irrelevance of U.S. Force Planning*, Carlisle Barracks, Pa.: Strategic Studies Institute, U.S. Army War College, May 19, 1998. As of January 17, 2018:
http://ssi.armywarcollege.edu/pdffiles/00300.pdf

Roxburgh, Charles, "The Use and Abuse of Scenarios," McKinsey and Company, November 2009. As of July 6, 2017:
http://www.mckinsey.com/business-functions/strategy-and-corporate-finance/our-insights/the-use-and-abuse-of-scenarios

Schnabel, James F., *The Joint Chiefs of Staff and National Policy*, Vol. I, *1945–1947*, Washington, D.C.: Joint Chiefs of Staff, Joint History Office, 1996.

———, *The Joint Chiefs of Staff and National Policy*, Vol. III, *1951–1953 The Korean War*, Part 2, Washington, D.C.: Joint Chiefs of Staff, Joint History Office, 1998.

Sherman, Jason, "Work Grabs Reins of Analysis Effort Pivotal to Strategy, Budget Decisions," *Inside Defense*, November 26, 2014.

Stevens, James G., "Perspectives on the Analysis M&S Community," briefing at U.S. Department of Defense modeling and simulation conference, Orlando, Fla., March 11, 2008. As of January 17, 2018:
http://www.dtic.mil/dtic/tr/fulltext/u2/a501001.pdf

Stevens, James G., and R. Eric Johnson, "Joint Data Support to the DoD Analytic Agenda," briefing at U.S. Military Academy, West Point, N.Y., June 21–23 2005. As of January 17, 2018:
http://www.dtic.mil/dtic/tr/fulltext/u2/a448559.pdf

Sweeney, Patrick C., *A Primer for: Guidance for Employment of the Force (GEF), Joint Strategic Capabilities Plan (JSCP), the Adaptive Planning and Execution (APEX) System, and Global Force Management*, Newport, R. I.: Joint Military Operations Department, U.S. Naval War College, July 29, 2011.

Troxell, John F., *Force Planning in an Era of Uncertainty: Two MRCs as a Force Sizing Framework*, Carlisle Barracks, Pa.: Strategic Studies Institute, U.S. Army War College, September 15, 1997.

U.S. Army War College, "Joint Strategic Capabilities Plan (JSCP)," webpage, undated. As of January 25, 2018:
https://ssl.armywarcollege.edu/dde/documents/jsps/terms/jscp.cfm

U.S. Department of Defense, *Data Collection, Development, and Management in Support of Strategic Analysis*, DoD Instruction 8260.1, December 2002, current as of December 2, 2003.

———, *Implementation of Data Collection, Development, and Management for Strategic Analyses*, DoD Instruction 8260.2, January 21, 2003.

———, *Support for Strategic Analysis*, DoD Instruction 8260.01, Washington, D.C., January 11, 2007.

———, *Joint Data Support (JDS)*, Washington, D.C., June 2009.

———, Support for Strategic Analysis (SSA), DoD Instruction 8260.05, Washington, D.C., July 7, 2011.

———, *Quadrennial Defense Review 2014*, Washington, D.C., March 4, 2014. As of June 26, 2017:
http://archive.defense.gov/pubs/2014_Quadrennial_Defense_Review.pdf

U.S. Government Accountability Office, *Quadrennial Defense Review: 2010 Report Addressed Many but Not All Required Items*, Washington, D.C., GAO-10-575R, April 30, 2010.

———, *Force Structure: Army's Analyses of Aviation Alternatives*, Washington, D.C., GAO-15-430R, April 27, 2015.

U.S. Naval War College, "Special Programs," webpage, undated. As of January 16, 2018:
https://usnwc2.usnwc.edu/Academics/Special-Programs.aspx

Watson, Robert J., *The Joint Chiefs of Staff and National Policy,* Vol. V, *1953–1954*, Washington, D.C.: Joint Chiefs of Staff, Joint History Office, 1986.

———, *The Joint Chiefs of Staff and National Policy,* Vol. III, *1950–1951 The Korean War,* Part I, Washington, D.C.: Joint Chiefs of Staff, Joint History Office, 1998.